Contents

Contents

Contents

About the author

James Barton has been Director of Studies and a careers adviser at Mander Portman Woodward's London college since September 2007. As well as being the author of *Getting into Veterinary School*, James has sat on interview and audition panels and has given careers advice across a range of fields.

Acknowledgements

I would like to thank James Burnett for all of his help and input in revising this edition of MPW's *Getting into Physiotherapy Courses*. I would also like to thank Lianne Carter and my family for their supportive words.

I would also like to reiterate the thanks given by the previous author to Alice Holmes, Fiona Pyrgos, Katherine Cran and Tania Dawson. I would especially like to extend my thanks to the Chartered Society of Physiotherapy for the enormous amount of information that they provided during the writing of this book.

The information in this book has come from a variety of sources and is, we believe, correct at the time of going to press. However, the views expressed are our own and any errors are down to us.

I hope that you find this book a valuable and educative tool and wish you all the success in your future endeavours in this field. Remember, life is what you make of it.

James Barton
October 2011
This book is for Gemma.

Warming up
Introduction

With eight minutes to go in a crucial match, you have to make a split-second choice. One option leads to potential glory, the other to probable defeat. One means winning at any cost, the other means counting the cost of defeat. Surely it is an easy decision, is it not? OK, so if you understand the reference, then this is an extreme example of the type of decision that physiotherapists have to make in their careers, but if you are not mindful of the choices that you make then the decisions you get wrong can often have bigger repercussions. A physiotherapist must be as patient as they are strict and as knowledgeable as they are honest, as rehabilitation is often the hardest part of any injury.

Most people associate physiotherapy with sport – even more so at the moment, and for all the wrong reasons. It is not uncommon on a Monday morning, when flicking through the back pages of the paper, to see that Johnny X is being assessed by the physiotherapist after having sustained a knock in the weekend's premiership encounter. And, of course, let us not forget the lore of the magic sponge in rugby or the tracksuited figure with the spray can designed to fix even the most gruesome of injuries. For others, physiotherapy is something that takes place after an accident, when the victim needs to learn to walk properly again. However, while physiotherapy encompasses both of these areas, there are many other facets to the profession and admissions tutors require you to be fully aware of that.

I was inspired to write this book after the application of one of my students. He did not get a place to study physiotherapy despite being a good candidate. He had a good personal statement and a lot of work experience but he focused too much on sport. This book will tell you about the importance of making sure you are not approaching this degree for that reason. Universities see straight through this. Physiotherapy is so much more than the glamour of sports clubs.

Physiotherapy is a competitive degree course. Last year, applications were up almost one fifth; 5,691 people applied to university to study physiotherapy, compared with 4,755 people in 2009 applying for 1,932 places.

The table over the page shows you approximately how many applicants there are per place.

Table 1: Number of applicants per place at university

University	Applicants per place (approx.)
Birmingham	9
Bradford	22
Brighton	30 (and 6 places for overseas students)
Bristol UWE	12
Brunel	11
Cardiff	17
Coventry	15
East Anglia	14
East London	10
Glasgow Caledonian	12
Hertfordshire	13
Huddersfield	18
King's College London	16
Kingston	9
Liverpool	20
Manchester	18
Northumbria	37
Queen Margaret	11
Robert Gordon	13
Salford	28
Sheffield Hallam	12
Southampton	15
Teesside	33
Ulster	12

What is physiotherapy?

The human body is a complex machine that can go wrong for any number of reasons. Physiotherapy is a science-based medical subject that looks in detail at how the body moves; how muscles, bones, joints and ligaments work and how they react to pain and trauma. Physiotherapists diagnose numerous ailments that affect the muscles and nerves, and then proceed to treat the patient, ensuring independence, movement and a return to maximum performance. It is the physiotherapist's job not only to look at the problem and treat it but also to look for any predisposing factors that may have contributed to the patient's ailment and to advise on how to minimise the risk of the same thing happening again.

Qualified physiotherapists work independently and as part of multidisciplinary teams, ensuring that patients' health and mobility are improved.

What do physiotherapists do?

Physiotherapists have numerous challenging roles within the health sector. They provide services such as rehabilitation and exercise before and after surgery. Within the wider community they provide services to adults with learning difficulties. They also have a role in the workplace where they can help to reduce injuries such as repetitive strain injury (RSI).

Chartered physiotherapists work with a wide range of people in many different environments, either individually or as part of a large healthcare team.

Physiotherapists deal with many different situations, including the following.

- Patient education. This is very important in physiotherapy and means teaching people the 'correct' way to move and lift in order to prevent or slow the onset of problems such as back pain or RSI (see Chapter 6). This may include helping athletes to avoid injury by discussing techniques and training programmes. Poor warm-up routines, too much training, poor equipment and incorrect technique are common causes of injuries, and all of them might be avoided. Using the idea that prevention is better than cure, physiotherapists are able to show people that very small changes will be hugely beneficial, for example good footwear or the use of a wrist support when using a computer.
- Helping women before and after pregnancy by advising them about posture and exercise.
- Helping children to deal with mental and physical disabilities.

- Developing the potential of people with learning difficulties through exercise, sport and recreation; this could also include the use of specialist equipment.
- Helping people to deal with stress and anxiety.
- Helping stroke victims recover movement in paralysed limbs.
- Helping orthopaedic patients after spinal operations or joint replacements and treating those debilitated following an accident. Using a variety of techniques to strengthen muscles and improve the mobility of individual joints, activities such as walking can be made much easier for people recovering from hip replacements or those with arthritis or osteoporosis. These methods can also reduce the pain and stiffness resulting from these conditions.
- Working with AIDS patients.
- Caring for those people who suffer from Parkinson's disease (one in 20 under the age of 40 has Parkinson's disease).
- Improving the confidence and self-esteem of those with mental illness through exercise and recreation, while also helping with relaxation and body awareness techniques.
- Working with the terminally ill (both inpatients and outpatients) or those in intensive care to maintain movement and prevent respiratory problems.
- Helping sportspeople recover from injury.
- Working in large businesses and companies to ensure that employees do not suffer from physical problems associated with their jobs.

Physiotherapists use a range of techniques, including:

- exercise
- hydrotherapy (see Chapter 11)
- infrared and ultraviolet radiation (see Chapter 11)
- manipulation
- massage
- ultrasound (see Chapter 11)
- vibration
- patient education
- movement analysis
- gait re-education (see Chapter 11)
- heat and cold application.

About this book

This book is structured very much like a standard physiotherapy session: it requires adequate warm-up, intensive drills and jumping through hoops, before finally seeing the finishing line, only to be given a leaflet detailing specific exercises for you to do at home. Stretch and challenge your mind without breaking your back!

How to use this book

The competition for places on approved degree courses is intense – there are very few university courses that have more applicants per place than physiotherapy. Physiotherapy courses receive more applicants per place than medicine, veterinary science or even courses at Oxford or Cambridge. Typically, a university might receive over 1,000 applications for 40 places. Even if each applicant makes five choices – and not all do – this still works out at around five students chasing every place. As you will see on page 21, the numbers are often far higher than this. With such intense competition for places you need to think carefully about all the stages of your application: from the preparation that you do before you apply through to the interview. You should also think about the steps you can take to maximise your chances of gaining a place should something go wrong at the examination stage.

This book is divided into five sections:

1. an explanation of what physiotherapists do
2. getting an interview
3. getting an offer
4. results day
5. useful information.

The first section outlines what physiotherapists do and looks at the kind of career you can expect as a physiotherapist. It also describes what the study of physiotherapy involves and the different course structures on offer. Please note that this book is designed to be a route map for potential physiotherapists rather than a comprehensive guide to physiotherapy as a profession. The Chartered Society of Physiotherapy, or physiotherapists you meet during work experience, should be the starting points for more detailed information on what being a physiotherapist entails.

The second section deals with the preparation that you need to undertake in order to make your application as strong as possible. It includes advice on work experience, how to choose a university, and the UCAS application itself.

The third section covers interviews, provides tips on what to expect and on how to ensure that you come across as a potential physiotherapist. It also contains a checklist for you to tick off the important steps in making your application.

The fourth section describes the steps that you need to take if you are holding an offer, or if you do not have an offer but want to gain a place through Clearing. On pages 69–72 there is advice and information for 'non-standard' applicants – mature students, graduates and retake students.

The final section provides useful information on fees and funding and details of the universities offering courses, including their entry requirements.

Entry requirements are quoted in terms of A level grades or UCAS points (the UCAS tariff) in this book. Information for students with Scottish Highers, the International Baccalaureate (IB), the BTEC National Diploma or the Irish Leaving Certificate is on page 71. The universities will be happy to provide you with further information on other qualifications.

At the end of the book there is a further information section and a glossary. Here you will find details of sources of further information on physiotherapy and definitions of any terms and abbreviations relevant to your UCAS application for physiotherapy courses.

For the latest news on physiotherapy and physiotherapy courses, go to www.mpw.co.uk/getintomed.

1 | Pressure points
Careers

It is essential that you are completely au fait with the essentials of physiotherapy before you apply to tertiary-level study; that includes knowing about the different career opportunities that the profession presents. The field you are hoping to enter is not a narrow one.

It is equally important that, when you qualify for the profession, you are quite entrepreneurial in your approach and progressive in terms of your thinking. Physiotherapists are in essence autonomous and therefore you have to consider the business elements of the profession. What this means is that physiotherapists make their own clinical judgements and treatment decisions and they also work in reflection, i.e. reviewing themselves and making corrections to their work where necessary.

Physiotherapy is a career that relies on the strength of the individual as well as the ability to work in a team. Physiotherapy as a subject is highly academic and therefore of great value; this means that employment prospects are large and varied. These prospects are not limited to the NHS; there is an enormous breadth of employment prospects that can be found across the different sectors (see page 10).

Physiotherapy is not, however, a profession that involves only physical therapy. Physiotherapists work with people – in most cases people who are disabled, or who have been ill or injured. Physiotherapists need to be able to communicate on a personal level with people of all ages; to be reassuring and comforting; to explain the treatments they are using; and to help patients overcome fear and pain.

Physiotherapists need to be able to assess the needs of their patients and to be aware of the effects of external circumstances such as social or cultural factors.

Working as a physiotherapist

Physiotherapists work in a range of health and care environments that include hospitals, the local community, private practice, industry and sports settings. The majority are employed by the NHS. Physiotherapy comprises the largest group within the allied healthcare professions with over 30,000 state-registered physiotherapists in the UK.

To qualify as a registered physiotherapist you need to gain an approved degree (see pages 79–80) that has been validated by the Chartered Society of Physiotherapy (CSP) and the Health Professions Council (HPC) – not the Council for Professions Supplementary to Medicine (CPSM), as used to be the case. If you complete the degree you are then eligible for state registration (State Registered Physiotherapist or SRP) and membership of the Chartered Society of Physiotherapy (MCSP, see Chapter 11).

Common career paths for physiotherapists

Once you have completed your BSc in Physiotherapy you will hopefully gain membership to the HPC and CSP, provided you have taken a course that is accredited by these organisations. To say there is a standard route is not correct. The main thing you need after graduating is clinical experience. The usual route would be to gain experience in areas you didn't cover on your placements in a rotational band 5 job.

A rotational band 5 job is a general physiotherapist role which will rotate around various departments, including respiratory, stroke, orthopaedic, etc. Each rotation will last around four months. These are commonly in the NHS or in some private practices and are designed to build up your expertise before you can qualify for the next band (band 6). These bands also equate to your pay scale, so more skills are vital.

A lot of physiotherapists get their rotational band 5 job through the NHS or by having impressed on their placements during their course. You do not have to work for the NHS first before going private. Some physiotherapists set up their own practices, but this is all based on reputation and having built up the relevant experience over many years. It is like anything in life, you have to prove yourself first.

Further qualifications are not essential after your degree but you are expected to maintain your CPD (continuing professional development), which is very important, as discussed below.

Private practice is one of the more lucrative career moves. Private practice as an umbrella term includes:

● treating patients independently for the same ailments as in the NHS
● working for a sports club or a specific team, aiding in the recovery of sportspersons from injury and helping to optimise their performance
● occupational rehabilitation, which means helping people to recover from accidents or illnesses and to return to their normal lives.

As you will discover later on in the book in Chapter 6, there are also additional opportunities to veer off on a tangent and get involved in policy development and research in order to ensure that physiotherapy as a profession continues to progress over the course of time in line with the NHS.

The areas of work available to you as an aspiring physiotherapist are outlined in Table 2.

Table 2: Areas of work for physiotherapists

Area	Work
Outpatients clinics	Advising and treating people with spinal and joint problems, or recovering from accidents and sports injuries
Patients in hospital	Treating inpatients, including people in intensive care units; helping very ill people: to keep their chests clear of secretions while they are too weak to cough effectively; to keep their limbs mobile while confined to bed
Schools	Working with teachers and parents in the support of children with developmental movement problems
Workplaces and industry	Advising managers and staff on injury prevention as well as treating specific problems
Sports and community centres	Promoting health and preventative health education through progressive exercise programmes and back-care classes
Women's health	Advising women on ante- and post-natal care; exercise and posture; managing continence (specialist physiotherapy can also help men with continence problems) following gynaecological operations
Elderly care	Maintaining mobility and independence; rehabilitation after falls; treating arthritis and Parkinson's disease
Stroke patients	Helping people with paralysed limbs to restore normal movement
Orthopaedics	Regaining movement and strength after spinal operations and hip, knee and other joint replacements; treating patients who have accidents and fractures
Mental illness	Holding relaxation and body awareness classes; improving confidence and self-esteem through exercise

Table 2: Continued

Area	Work
People with learning difficulties	Developing people's potential through sports and recreation; assessing and providing specialist footwear, seating and equipment
Terminally ill people	Supporting people with end of life conditions in the community or in hospices
Private sector	Working independently in private practice, clinics, hospitals and GP surgeries, treating a wide range of conditions
Voluntary organisations	Providing expertise and advice in organisations that support people with conditions such as multiple sclerosis and Parkinson's disease
Community	Going into people's homes and providing a service for those not able to attend a clinic – this area of work is developing as a result of changes in the NHS and is more common nowadays

Table reproduced with permission of the Chartered Society of Physiotherapy, November 2011, www.csp.org.uk.

Employment prospects

'Newly qualified physiotherapists looking for jobs now are in a much better position than their colleagues who graduated in the past couple of years.'

Quote from the CSP (2011) (www.csp.org.uk)

In the last edition of this book, the figures were not so favourable for graduates. At that time, a survey by the CSP revealed that of the 2,000 or so physiotherapy graduates who left university in 2005, about 53% did not have jobs to go to after graduation. The Hospital Episode Statistics for 2003/04 revealed the need for more NHS physiotherapists, and the CSP said: 'Over half a million people with injuries were admitted to an NHS hospital in England last year.' However, the picture is no longer as bleak as it seemed then, with most physiotherapy graduates finding relevant employment and, once you have a job, promotion prospects are good, with many vacancies at senior level.

According to Prospects.ac.uk, the number of employed physiotherapy graduates has risen by 7.4% from the previous year, showing a slight improvement in the situation. In the UK, 68% of physiotherapy graduates from 2007 were working as physiotherapists six months after graduation. If you compare that with the 64.6% in 2006, you can see this positive improvement. There was also a 3.6% drop in unemployment to 4.3% in 2007.

More recent research by the CSP has shown that there are increasing numbers of graduates finding employment as junior physiotherapists, on either permanent or short-term contracts. This growth is increasing on a yearly basis. The CSP workforce review shows that:

- in 2006, 31% of students had found work as a junior physiotherapist
- in 2007, 53% of students had found work as a junior physiotherapist
- in 2008, 60% of students had found work as a junior physiotherapist
- in 2010, 80% of students had found work as a junior physiotherapist.

N.B. This percentage is likely to have increased since the 2010 figures were published.

According to the CSP, the physiotherapy workforce has 'undergone significant growth over recent years', having increased by 41% between 2000 and 2009. The HPC recorded 44,734 registered physiotherapists as of January 2010.

What is important to note is that significantly more physiotherapists are registered with the HPC than with the NHS. Some 7,300 CSP members work exclusively outside the NHS (for example in private hospitals, sports clubs or their own private practice). New government policy has increased private sector healthcare provision and so more physiotherapists are now employed outside the NHS.

In terms of the age and gender split of the workforce, the NHS has 84% female to 16% male physiotherapists. The CSP reports that more men train to be physiotherapists, leading to the conclusion that they are more likely to work outside the NHS, and over half were mature students. There is also a relatively young age profile for physiotherapists, which means that there is not likely to be an imminent surge in retirements.

While there is no data for 2011 yet, it should be noted that the recession will possibly have had a negative impact on employment rates.

You can maximise your chances of employment by studying a degree accredited by the CSP and HPC (which replaced the CPSM) and also by being a student member.

Continuing professional development (CPD)

Throughout their careers, physiotherapists are expected to develop their skills and to keep up to date with developments within the field in a structured and systematic way. This is known as CPD. Physiotherapists are responsible for identifying, planning and recording their own CPD, setting themselves targets and collecting evidence in a portfolio to support their CPD. The process of CPD is summarised in Figure 1.

Figure 1: Process of continuing professional development (CPD)

Occupational therapy

While there are a number of differences between physiotherapy and occupational therapy, a lot of similarities are also found. The link is often between dealing with the physical and the mental faculties of a patient in order to ensure their overall rehabilitation. Occupational therapists help people to carry out the tasks and activities that are necessary for them to lead a fulfilling life. These might be work related – helping people with disabilities to cope with their jobs – or they might be everyday things like cooking, bathing, travelling or socialising. Occupational therapists work in hospitals, for charities and social organisations, in schools and the workplace, in prisons, within the local community, and in many other situations. Occupational therapists deal with physical, mental and social needs, for example:

- helping children deal with learning difficulties
- helping people with mental illness to look after themselves, or to be successful in their jobs
- working with accident victims to enable them to re-learn physical tasks
- advising businesses about how to adapt facilities and premises to enable people with disabilities to cope with their jobs
- creating rehabilitation programmes for refugees or the homeless.

To practise as an occupational therapist, it is necessary to follow a degree course in occupational therapy which has been approved by the HPC and accredited by the College of Occupational Therapists (COT).

For UK students, the tuition fees for the degree course are normally paid by the NHS. Contact details for the COT and other useful organisations can found on pages 82–83.

> 'Physiotherapy appealed to me because it was a practical job, rather than being academically based. I had always been interested in science and biology in particular, and come from a medical background. I had seen both my parents treat patients in different ways and get great satisfaction from it, and I felt it was something I wanted to do.'
>
> Katherine, University of Hertfordshire

2 | Strengthen your core
Physiotherapy courses: what to expect

This chapter deals with the types of course that you can expect at university. It looks at a typical structure of the BSc as well as the different teaching approaches you might find. It also discusses courses in Scotland, Wales and Northern Ireland and the differences in course style as well as MSc (pre-registration) courses. It is useful to note that these are guidelines and that courses can vary between universities, so make sure you research the course properly.

Typical course structure

While all physiotherapy courses contain many common elements, there are significant differences in the structure of these courses, in the course content, in the way in which the practical and patient-contact elements are arranged, and in the styles of assessment. You should investigate this thoroughly by reading prospectuses and looking at the physiotherapy departments' websites in order to find out which ones will suit you best.

A typical course structure will look something like the following.

First year

Underlying theory and practical issues:

- anatomy
- cardiovascular and respiratory functions
- communication and clinical skills
- kinesiology (the mechanics of body movement)
- musculoskeletal conditions
- physiology
- research methods.

Second year

The second-year course divides the time between academic study and clinical placements:

- clinical education, taking into account social, cultural and economic factors

- clinical placements
- neurology
- pathophysiology.

Clinical placements take place in a variety of settings, including hospital wards, physiotherapy outpatient departments and specialised units within hospitals and the community. The clinical placements will focus on areas such as orthopaedics, rehabilitation and community medicine. CSP guidelines require a certain number of hours (1,000) of clinical practice to be undertaken in order to gain recognition, and the 16 weeks of clinical placement usually comprise around 30 hours per week.

Third year

The third year will also be split between clinical and academic study – students will usually spend about 20 weeks of the course on clinical placements. Specialist areas of study could include:

- burns and plastic surgery
- exercise and sports science
- learning difficulties
- mental health
- neurology
- neurorehabilitation
- outpatients
- paediatrics
- pain management
- respiratory medicine.

Research dissertation

There will be continuing modules in research alongside the clinical placements. Evidence-based practice is essential in physiotherapy, therefore students need to learn how to carry out research as well as how to use existing research. For all honours degrees, this is a major component of the course in the second and third years, and there is a focus towards a final research dissertation that will be submitted in the final year. This will refine the research skills you have learnt during your three-year course and allow you to demonstrate your knowledge on a relevant topic of your choice.

Elective clinical placement

At the end of the third year there might be an elective clinical placement. You will choose the specialty in which you wish to work and arrange the placement yourself. Many students choose to work abroad, or in areas of healthcare not previously encountered in their own clinical education.

Be aware of the different teaching styles of the course and refer to the universities' websites to find out all the information. Some courses are modular, some have a lot of emphasis on clinical teaching, and others are more theoretical. You need to find out which one utilises your skills.

Teaching styles

These will be different depending on the instructor and the course material; however, they can broadly be split into the following types.

- **Interactive:** An interactive style is what the name implies, with discussions, Q&A sessions and presentations. This style suits those who have already absorbed the facts, and therefore students will look into the facts themselves and build on them through the practical aspects of the course.
- **Lecture:** A lecture is useful for providing a lot of facts in one session which will then be researched further outside the course. This implies extra reading to supplement what you have been taught.
- **Problem-based learning (PBL):** This is student-centered learning where you will learn about topics by looking at multifaceted and realistic problems. You will work in groups and identify what you know, what you need to know and how you will find the information necessary for solving the problems. The instructor will ask questions and provide resources to lead you to the right answers. However, you must figure them out for yourself.
- **Practice-based professional learning (PBPL):** This style requires a level of professional practice in order to fully understand the course. It is in contrast to theory-led learning and is directly related to the practical aspects of the course. It is a new style of learning and is prevalent in the newer universities.

You should look on the websites for the individual universities to find out which teaching style they use. See Chapter 10 for university contact details.

Courses in Scotland

There are three universities in Scotland where you can study physiotherapy:

1. Queen Margaret University
2. Glasgow Caledonian University
3. Robert Gordon University.

These are four years full time instead of three years full time as in England. The courses have a strong clinical bias with work placements and you are required to complete an honours project in your fourth year.

Robert Gordon University even has a three-dimensional modelling approach to learning as well, which makes the course more interactive.

There is also the option of taking a two-year MSc in Physiotherapy pre-registration course or an equivalent MSc in Rehabilitation Science accelerated course after taking a different degree. This allows students another opportunity to study physiotherapy after having been taught the necessary course in a different and unrelated discipline.

The section below summarises the options on offer on the Scottish courses so that you can see the different approaches of a Scottish university. Apart from the length of course, you will see that they are not wholly dissimilar to the English courses.

Queen Margaret University

Years one and two are spent learning the basic and applied sciences needed for physiotherapy, as well as developing patient management and therapeutic skills. Part of your learning will be alongside an experienced, registered physiotherapist, working with patients, carers and/or families. It is important to work with other health and social care professionals to see the role each one plays in a patient's care. Practice-based learning is employed in settings around Scotland; this is funded by you.

In the final year, you will work in small groups to undertake a relevant project to enhance your skills for work.

The university has implemented an inter-professional education (IPE) focus to allow an autonomous and team-based approach. This will develop your all-round skills, teamwork, strategy and confidence as well as allowing you the chance to learn from professionals.

Glasgow Caledonian University

The aim of this course is to give you the professional and academic knowledge and skills needed to manage individual patients. This course promotes your critical analysis and you will have to use this to justify and evaluate evidence in your practical work. This will be particularly relevant in your honours project in your fourth year. Different models of care will be discussed, and you will gain an understanding of the influence of governmental policy on the profession. Healthy lifestyles and physical activity are promoted heavily on this course and placements play a big part in supplementing your learning.

Robert Gordon University

A very modern course, this is designed to help you 'meet the demands of the rapidly changing health sector'. The clinical placement is of primary importance as it gives you the 'real' experiences that will ensure your professional credibility.

This is very much a practical course in state-of-the-art teaching and clinical skills facilities. You will use practical therapy rooms and a human performance laboratory. There is also a 'sophisticated three-dimensional motion analysis system' which will allow you to see in action what it is you are being taught. There is also a unique computerised 'SimMan' in the clinical skills area where you will be able to practise before going into a real-life setting.

Courses in Wales

The section below summarises the options on offer at Cardiff University.

Cardiff University

The department is over 100 years old and offers a CSP-accredited degree over three years. The diversity and complexity of the profession are mirrored by the theory and practice elements on this course. It combines university lectures with 'a minimum of 1,000 hours of placement education'. You will learn from both academic and clinic physiotherapists, creating a holistic approach. Students gain experience in all of the core areas of the profession. Placements take place around Wales but might also be arranged in other locations in order to maintain high standards.

Courses in Northern Ireland

In Northern Ireland there is one principal university of recognition teaching the physiotherapy course, the University of Ulster. One key difference is its use of peer examination. Like the other universities discussed above, the split is between theory and practice, but a large emphasis is placed on practice-based learning. You will have to take the Health Professions Admission Test (HPAT) in order to gain a place at the university. The HPAT is the exam used by the Irish Medical Schools. The test is written and assesses a student's logical, reasoning and problem-solving skills. Non-verbal reasoning is also marked, as is a student's clarity of their own thought and the thoughts of others.

University of Ulster

In each year of the programme, you will usually take six modules, including inter-professional modules. A feature of this course is the integration of theory and practice; participation is expected from everyone and peer examination is used as a testing device. The University of Ulster uses practice-based learning. From your first year onwards, you will take part in five placements throughout your course to help confirm your learning. Travel and accommodation costs are handled by the student.

MSc (pre-registration) course

This is different to the postgraduate MSc in Physiotherapy. This is for those who have not trained as a physiotherapist yet and have a degree in another relevant subject. A postgraduate MSc is for students who have already trained as a physiotherapist and now want to specialise. This course is arguably even more competitive than the BSc entry. The MSc (pre-registration course) is a two-year, full-time qualifying pro-gramme for graduates with a suitable and relevant first degree.

The course aims to give students with the necessary skills a second opportunity to take on evidence-based physiotherapy programmes with a variety of patients. A large emphasis is placed on the implementation of research and auditing programmes. This course is accredited by the CSP and the HPC.

Course overview

The course is divided between research and clinical placements. A large emphasis is placed on the latter, which is typically arranged over six modules with over 1,000 hours of study. Students will treat patients and watch professionals in different settings, from in-house to home visits. There are three core areas – the management of neurological, cardio-pulmonary and neuromusculoskeletal dysfunctions – with knowledge from the biomedical and psycho-social sciences recruited as required.

First year

The first year develops practice and reasoning in the core areas of prac-tice. Evaluation and critical analysis are key to development in terms of physiotherapeutic concepts. In the last part of the year students begin their research project.

Second year

The clinical modules and research project continue during the second year. There will also be work on an Advancing Physiotherapy module, which addresses other approaches to the management of physiotherapy.

3 | On the rack/under observation
The UCAS application

In order to gain a place at university you have to submit a UCAS application. Before you do this, however, you need to be sure that you have investigated physiotherapy as thoroughly as you can. You need to do this for two reasons:

1. you must be sure that physiotherapy is the right career for you
2. you must demonstrate to the university admissions tutors that you are aware of the demands of the profession.

With so many applicants for every university place, the selectors need to be sure that they do not 'waste' a place on someone who will then drop out of the course or the profession. For this reason the application has to be very convincing. Most people's exposure to physiotherapy is limited, and so you need to investigate the profession in depth.

Making your application stand out

When your UCAS application is received by the university it will not be on its own but in a batch of, possibly, several hundred. The selectors will have to consider it, along with the others, in between the demands of their 'real' jobs. If your application is uninteresting, lacking evidence of real commitment to physiotherapy, or badly worded, it will be put on the reject pile. Nottingham University, for example, receives more than 1,600 applications for its 50 places. From these, about 300 people are interviewed.

You can only be called for interview on the basis of your UCAS application. The selectors will not know about the things that you have forgotten to say and they can only get an impression of you from what is in the application. We have come across too many good students who never got an interview simply because they did not think about the UCAS application; they relied on the hope that the selectors would somehow see through the words and get an instinctive feeling about them. The following sections will tell you more about what the selectors are looking for, and how you can avoid common mistakes. Before looking at how the selectors go about deciding whom to call for interview, however, there are a number of important things that you need to think about.

> 'When we interview students, we want to find out two things –
> whether they are really committed to the profession, and whether
> they have the right personality to succeed. For the first of these,
> it is work experience, work experience, work experience that mat-
> ters. For the second, I look for the ability to respond to my ques-
> tions calmly and with structure. I also look at whether they have
> contributed to the life of their school, college or community.'
>
> Admissions tutor

Work experience

According to Nottingham University's physiotherapy website:

> 'Physiotherapy is a vocational degree and applicants need to
> be enthusiastic about the profession and sure in their own minds
> that they really want to be a physiotherapist. We require you to
> undertake as much physiotherapy work experience as possible
> primarily within the NHS hospital and community settings before
> applying. Experience in other areas, such as special schools,
> private practice, sports clinics, and centres for the elderly will
> strengthen your application. It is important to note that without
> work experience it is likely that your application will be rejected.'
>
> Nottingham University

Work experience is vital if you are to be considered. Without evidence that you have worked with people in the community, preferably within the NHS, you will not be offered a place. Although not all universities are as explicit as Nottingham, most will emphasise the need for work experience. For example, Brunel University's website (www.brunel.ac.uk) says that all applicants are advised to undertake a period of observationary physiotherapy clinical experience with a chartered physiotherapist.

Although work-shadowing physiotherapists in specialist areas such as sports clinics or private practices is useful experience it is generally not enough, and applicants without some contact with NHS hospitals are likely to find it hard to get an interview or an offer. If you are very lucky (and very determined) you may be able to get a paid job in an NHS hospital as a physiotherapy assistant. However, because of school or college commitments, this is usually only possible during a gap year. It is more likely that you will have to settle for an unpaid volunteer position either on a part-time basis (at weekends or in the evenings) or for a short period of time in the school holidays.

If you are unable to arrange either of these you should try to shadow a physiotherapist for a day or two, and supplement this with a volunteer job in another caring environment such as an old people's home, a hospice or the children's ward of your local hospital.

Length of time

While there are no rules about the minimum length of time that you should spend doing work experience, volunteer work or work-shadowing, as a general rule the candidates who can demonstrate commitment by doing something on a regular basis throughout the year or who have spent at least two weeks in a hospital environment are likely to be in the strongest position. In the current economic climate this will be difficult. Think outside the box and volunteer in hospices, schools or old people's homes and watch the nurses and physiotherapists there. You can also chat to physiotherapists or go to physiotherapy appointments with friends or relatives.

> 'Get as much experience as you can – it doesn't just have to be as a physiotherapy assistant. Be determined: there is always a way to get in if you really want to.'
>
> Katherine, University of Hertfordshire

Some schools operate schemes where they arrange this for you. This saves you the hard work of contacting hospitals or clinics, but the disadvantage is that you will be unable to impress the selectors with your dynamism and determination because you will not be able to say 'I arranged my work experience myself'.

If your school does not operate such a scheme you have two options: to use any contacts that your family or friends have, or to approach local hospitals. To do the latter you need to get the names and addresses of local hospitals with physiotherapy departments and physiotherapy clinics from the internet. One such website is www.physiotherapyworkexperience.co.uk. You should send an email and include the name of a referee, someone who can vouch for your interest in physiotherapy as well as for your reliability. Your careers teacher, housemaster or housemistress or form teacher would be ideal. An example of a suitable email is given below.

From: Lucy Johnson
To: volunteers@melchesterhospital.org
Subject: Volunteer work

Dear Sir/Madam
I am in the first year of my A level studies and I am interested in a career in physiotherapy. In order to find out more about

physiotherapy I would like to work as a volunteer in the physio-therapy department. I would be able to work on Wednesday after-noons, Saturday afternoons and all day Sunday for the rest of this year. I would be extremely grateful if you would be prepared to meet me, in order to discuss whether it would be possible for me to spend some time at Melchester General Hospital.

If you require a reference, please contact my careers teacher. His name and address are:
Mr N Townson
Head of Careers
Melchester High School
Melchester
MC1 2CD

I look forward to hearing from you.
Yours sincerely
Lucy Johnson

As well as helping you to decide whether you are serious about physio-therapy and adding weight to your application, work experience is useful because you may be able to get one of the people you work with to give you a reference, which you could send in support of your UCAS applica-tion or produce at your interview.

Work experience in Wales

It is very difficult if not impossible to get work experience in NHS Wales if you are under 18. Cardiff University therefore does not stipulate work experience as being essential but the university does want to see that applicants have spoken to physiotherapists or physiotherapy students, that they have looked at physiotherapy-related publications and they have contacted the CSP (which has a pretty comprehensive careers page).

Things to look out for during work experience

The variety of treatments available to patients

Make sure that you know what you are observing. Ask the physiothera-pist or nurse for the technical names of the procedures that you see, and for information on the techniques and equipment used. Ask about the advantages and disadvantages of different types of treatments, and in what situations they are used. Keep a diary of what you saw on a day-to-day basis so that you can use it to revise from before an interview. There are a number of websites that provide detailed information on medical conditions and treatments, and you could add further detail to your diary using one of these. The addresses are at the end of the book.

Working as a physiotherapist

Ask the physiotherapist about his or her life. Find out about the hours, how much physiotherapists are paid, the demands of the job and the career options open to physiotherapists. Find out what the physiotherapists like about the job, and what they dislike.

Case study: Adam, first year student at Nottingham

Adam first thought of physiotherapy as a possible career when he realised that he was never going to play cricket for England. 'It was never a realistic option because I was never very good at cricket, but I loved sport and I wanted to be involved in it. By the time I was 13 I realised that, if I couldn't make the school team, I certainly wouldn't get a call from England!

'I got two A grades at GCSE and the rest were Bs and Cs. I decided to take Biology, Economics and Sports Science for A level, and Physics as an AS level. I found them hard but I knew that I needed BBB to get into Nottingham, my first choice. Someone at school told me that I had to get work experience so I arranged to shadow the physiotherapist at my local football team for three days. Just before I applied I went to an open day and was told that I would probably be rejected because my work experience was insufficient. My form teacher's wife worked at a hospital nearby so she was able to get me into the physiotherapy department there as an assistant very quickly. If I hadn't been to the open day, and been lucky that I had a contact in an NHS physiotherapy department, I wouldn't even have been interviewed.'

Adam's interviews concentrated on his work experience: 'They really probed me about what being a physiotherapist is really like – not just what I did, but what it is like working as a physiotherapist day in and day out, so I'm glad I did it.' Adam received two offers from his four physiotherapy choices. He was not confident about the grades he was going to get, so he put down two other choices – sports science and sports management – where the grade requirements were lower. The work experience convinced him that he desperately wanted to become a physiotherapist. 'I didn't really know what physiotherapy was about, even though I had applied to study it, before I did my work experience. I thought that it was a glamorous job where you worked with sportsmen, got to see sport for free, and spent most of the day chatting about sport.

The spell in the hospital showed me what it really entails. Dealing with stroke victims, or old people who do not know what is happening to them, is not easy. You need lots of patience and to really want to make a difference to them. I will probably end up working in a sport-related environment, but I am more open-minded now than I was before.'

Adam achieved AAB, higher than the grades that he needed, and is now in his first year at Nottingham.

Be aware that you should not apply for different courses on your form. You will be rejected straight away if you put four physiotherapy choices and one for a subject such as nursing or podiatry. This does not show a real commitment to physiotherapy. With such large numbers of students to look at, this is one criteria that will be used to reject applicants.

Tips for work experience

- Dress as the physiotherapists dress: be clean, tidy and reasonably formal. There are no strict rules here. You should dress professionally – some wear a shirt and tie, in sports physiotherapy you might wear shorts and a polo shirt, and hospitals have their own specific uniforms. Use your common sense!
- Offer to help the physiotherapist or the nurses with routine tasks.
- Show an interest in everything that is going on around you.

'My mother worked as an occupational therapist and so I was able to gain extended experience in four major hospitals in the London area. This was absolutely invaluable to me in showing me I wanted to study physiotherapy. This experience was divided between working in mental health and working in the community in order to get a real feeling for getting information across and working as part of a team.'

Trevor, Bristol UWE

Choice of university

Once you have completed your work experience, and are sure that you want to be a physiotherapist, you need to research your choice of university. There are various factors that you should take into account:

- the type of course

- the entrance requirements (see pages 79–80)
- location
- whether you would be taught alongside students on other health-care courses such as radiology, nursing, occupational therapy or podiatry.

Research

The first thing to do is to get hold of the prospectuses. If your school does not have spare copies, telephone the universities; they will send you copies free of charge. All universities have very informative web-sites that carry extra information on admissions policies. Once you have narrowed down the number of universities to, say, seven or eight, you should try to visit them in order to get a better idea of what studying there would be like. Your school careers department will have details of open days (or you could telephone the universities directly), and some universities will arrange for you to be shown around at other times of the year as well.

> **TIP!**
>
> Do not simply select your universities because someone tells you that they have good reputations or that they are easier to get into, because you will be spending the next three or four years of your life at one of them, and if you do not like the place you are unlikely to last the course.

Apart from talking to current or former physiotherapy students or careers advisers, there are a number of other sources of information. The *Guardian* newspaper publishes its own league table of universities, ranked by a total score that combines the university's teaching assessment, a 'value added' score based on the class of degree obtained compared with A level (or equivalent) grades, spending on facilities and materials, student/staff ratios, job prospects and entrance requirements. *The Times* also compiles its own table. The *Guardian*'s tables can be found at http://education.guardian.co.uk/universityguide.

Of course, league tables tell you only a small part of the whole story, and anyone who makes their choices solely on this basis without visiting the universities or reading the prospectuses is taking a serious risk.

Open days

Making your choice of university should not be approached without going to the open days of the universities where you are thinking about applying. It also gives you the opportunity to ask an admissions tutor any questions that you might have about the university generally, such as about sporting activities, societies or accommodation. You should go with a list of questions and show yourself to be proactive. After all, you would not go shopping and buy clothes without trying them on! Details can be found on the university websites.

Try to go to as many as you can, providing you are allowed to by your school. If you cannot attend the open day, go and have a look on a different day and email any questions you have to the admissions tutor. Do not ask questions that you can find out for yourself on the website, such as 'What is the grade requirement?'; this does not show you to be proactive, just lazy. Ask for details not generics.

Academic requirements

In addition to the grades required at A level and AS level, all of the universities specify the minimum grades that they require at GCSE. This varies from university to university, but it is unlikely that you will be considered unless you have at least five or six GCSEs, including science, English and mathematics, taken at one sitting and at grade A/B or above (check specific university websites for the exact requirements). If your grades fall below these requirements you need to get your referee to comment on them, to explain either why you underperformed (illness, family disruption, etc.) or why they expect your A level performance to be better than your GCSE grades indicate.

AS levels

Students following the A level system should also work hard to ensure that they gain good grades at AS level. Remember that how well you do is important from the start, since not only do AS grades appear on the form but many universities and medical schools will specify minimum grades needed, and may even ask for module breakdowns. Even those that do not have an explicit AS grade requirement will consciously or unconsciously use them as an indicator of your likely A level grades.

Imagine the situation: the selector has one more interview slot to fill, and has the choice between two students with identical work experience, GCSE results and A level predictions; however, one has scored DDDD at AS level, and the other achieved AAAA. Who do you think will get the interview?

The other thing to bear in mind is that a score of DDDD is unlikely to lead to BBB at A level, since an AS contributes 50% of the total A level marks, and so the selectors may doubt that the predicted grades are achievable. What this information will do is give admissions tutors more to go on than GCSE grades and A level predictions alone, since the AS grades will be published in the August preceding your application and can feature on your UCAS application. It is possible that most universities will specify a minimum AS level requirement for applicants. For the student, this means that the first year of A levels is as important as the second, and the days of the lower sixth being seen as a relaxed year are over.

The importance of your AS levels cannot be understated.

As the AS scores contribute half of the marks that make up the A level, you should try to re-sit any weak AS units in the second year of your A levels. This can be done in January or June.

Coursework can also make a big difference to the final grade – make sure that you are fully aware of the examination boards' requirements before submitting coursework.

An understanding of a subject does not mean that you will gain a high grade at AS or A level, as the examiners have very specific requirements. Specimen mark schemes can be found on the examination boards' websites (see page 83 for details).

Entrance requirements

Entrance requirements vary from university to university, but a 'standard' offer might ask for a minimum of 320 points from three A levels, including three 4/6-unit awards or equivalent. The offer would probably specify that biology must be studied to A2 level, along with one other science. A* grades are not usually asked for but do represent higher points. It is most common that you will be given an offer based on getting three grades as opposed to points. It is worthwhile checking your offer conditions when they are through to check whether points are also accepted.

This offer of 320 points would be satisfied by a student who gained BBB at A level (6-unit awards) and E at AS level (3-unit award). However, this is not the case for all universities.

You should also check the university prospectuses for details of A level and AS level requirements. Some universities, for example, specify that they require one of the AS subjects to be an arts subject or humanity, rather than them all being science subjects or mathematics.

Your choices

There are five spaces in the UCAS application, all of which may be used for physiotherapy courses. (In contrast, students applying for medicine, dentistry or veterinary science may use only four of their five choices on these courses.) You do not have to fill all five spaces with physiotherapy courses. You are allowed to apply for a mixture of physiotherapy courses and non-physiotherapy courses, or to leave spaces blank.

If you are worried that you might not be offered a place to study physiotherapy and you would consider other courses, you might want to put down four physiotherapy courses and one other course. The one non-physiotherapy course should be related to physiotherapy, either directly (occupational therapy, podiatry) or in a related discipline such as human biology, physiology, radiology or nursing. You should not enter fewer than four physiotherapy courses in the application because if you do you are unlikely to convince the selectors that you are genuinely committed.

TIP!

Whatever you do, be careful about putting down medicine or veterinary science as your other choices, because it will be obvious to the selectors that you are not committed to physiotherapy. Equally, if you want to apply for medicine, including a physiotherapy course on your form will be seen as a lack of commitment to medicine.

If you decide that you would be happy to accept an alternative to physiotherapy if you are unsuccessful, by all means choose another course as long as you feel able to justify the choice at interview. However, our advice is to apply only to physiotherapy courses because:

- it demonstrates to the selectors that you are committed to becoming a physiotherapist
- you do not run the risk of feeling obliged to accept a place on a course that at heart you do not wish to take – if you are unsuccessful in your initial application for physiotherapy you might be able to gain a place through Clearing, if you accept no alternative offers
- the more places you apply to, the more chances you are giving yourself.

Once you have made your final choices make sure that you have entered the details into the application correctly. More advice on this can be found in *How to Complete Your UCAS Application* (Trotman, 2012).

The personal statement

This is the most important part of your application, as this is where you convince the selectors that you are a serious and suitable candidate. Advice on writing your personal statement is given in the next chapter.

The reference

As well as your results and your personal statement, the selectors will take your reference into account. This is where your head, housemaster or housemistress or head of sixth form writes about what an outstanding person you are, the life and soul of the school; how you are on target for three A grades at A level; and why you will become an outstanding physiotherapist. For him or her to say this, of course, it has to be true.

The referee is expected to be as honest as possible, and to try to accurately assess your character and potential. You may believe that you have all of the qualities, academic and personal, necessary in a physiotherapist, but unless you have demonstrated these to your teachers they will be unable to support your application. Ideally your efforts to impress them will have begun at the start of the sixth form (or before); you will have become involved in school activities, you will have been working hard at your studies and you will be popular with students and teachers alike. However, it is never too late, and some people mature later than others, so if this does not sound like you, start to make efforts now to impress the people who will contribute to your reference.

As part of the reference your referee will need to predict the grades that you are likely to achieve. As you will see from Table 4 on pages 79–80, most universities ask for at least ABB. If your predicted grades are lower than this it is unlikely that you will be considered. Talk to your teachers and find out whether you are on target for these grades. If not, you need to:

● work harder or more effectively – and make sure that your teachers notice that you are doing so, or
● get some extra help either at school or outside, for instance by taking an Easter revision course, or
● delay submitting your UCAS application until you have your A level results. If you decide on this option make sure that you use your gap year wisely (see below).

When to submit the UCAS application

The closing date for receipt of the application by UCAS is 15 January.

Late applications are accepted by UCAS but the universities are not obliged to consider them. Because of the pressure on places, it is unlikely that late applications will be considered. Although you can submit your application any time between the beginning of September and the January deadline (remembering to get it to your referee at least two weeks before the deadline so that he or she has time to prepare the reference), most admissions tutors admit that the earlier the application is submitted the better your chance of being called for interview. Your best bet is to talk to the person who will deal with the application in the summer term of your first year of A levels, and work on your personal statement and choice of universities over the summer holidays so that the application is ready to hand in at the start of the September term.

'I chose St George's because it offered early and very good clinical contact and training alongside other healthcare professionals, and because they were the most helpful prior to submitting my application. I was really glad that I spent a long time studying the prospectuses, looking at websites, talking to physiotherapy students, coaches, admissions tutors and advisers at my college because I then was able to make a very informed decision about the most suitable course for me.'

Alice, St George's

Deferred entry

Most admissions tutors are happy to consider students who take a gap year, and many encourage it. However, if you are considering this, you need to make sure that you are going to use the time constructively. A year spent watching daytime TV is not going to impress anybody, whereas independent travelling, charity or voluntary work either at home or abroad, work experience or a responsible job will all indicate that you have used the time to develop independence and maturity. Above all, make sure that whatever you do with the year involves regular contact with other people.

You can either apply for deferred entry when you submit your UCAS application, in which case you need to outline your plans in your personal statement, or apply in the September following the publication of your A level results. If you expect to achieve your predicted grades and the feedback from your school or college is that you will be given a good reference, you should apply for deferred entry; but if you are advised by your referee that you are unlikely to be considered, you should give yourself more time to work on your referees by waiting until you have your A level results.

What happens next?

You can follow the progress of your application using the UCAS online Track system, which will show you when your form was sent to the universities and their responses.

The next correspondence you will receive, if you are lucky, is likely to be from the universities, asking you to attend an interview. Do not be alarmed if you do not hear anything soon after UCAS has sent you your statement of entry. Some universities interview on a first-come, first-served basis while others wait until all applications are in before deciding who to interview.

If you are unlucky you will receive a message from UCAS telling you that you have been rejected by one or more of the universities. Do not despair; you may hear better news from another of the places that you applied to. Even if you get five rejections, the worst thing that you can do is give up and decide that it is no longer worth working hard. On the contrary, if this does happen, you should become even more determined to gain high grades so that you can apply either through Clearing or the following year. The process of making Clearing applications is discussed on pages 63–65.

Application timescale

Year 12

- Organise work experience.
- Order prospectuses.
- Go to open days.

Year 13

- **September:** Complete your application and send it off to UCAS – it will be accepted from 1 September onwards.
- **15 January:** Deadline for submitting your applications to UCAS. They will consider late applications, but your chances are limited since some of the places will have gone already.
- **February–April:** Interviews may be held.
- **March:** If you have been rejected by all of your choices, you can enter UCAS Extra, a scheme that allows you to apply to other universities. Contact UCAS (www.ucas.com) for details.
- **April:** Decisions will begin to go directly to the candidates. When you have received all of the decisions, UCAS will send you a deadline by which you must choose one course as your firm acceptance and a second one (usually with a lower grade requirement) as your insurance choice.
- **Results day:** If you got the grades, congratulations! If you missed your grades, you need to look at your Clearing options. Clearing starts straight away so do not waste any time – get hold of a list of unfilled places and contact the universities direct. You will be sent instructions on Clearing automatically. UCAS has now introduced a new scheme called Adjustment which allows students who have performed significantly better than they had expected a short period

to approach universities that require higher grades than the offer they were holding.

Application checklist

- At least two weeks of NHS work-shadowing?
- Voluntary work?
- Right GCSE subjects and grades?
- Right A level subjects?
- On target for required grades?
- Looked at all the universities' prospectuses?
- Open days?
- Minimum of four physiotherapy choices in the UCAS application?
- Personal statement demonstrates commitment, research, personal qualities, communication skills and manual dexterity?

For more details about UCAS and filling in your application, see *How to Complete Your UCAS Application* (Trotman, 2012).

4| Tweak it
The personal statement

The personal statement is your opportunity to demonstrate to the selectors that you have not only researched physiotherapy thoroughly, but also have the right personal qualities to succeed as a physiotherapist. There are some universities that do not interview students and therefore they need to see all the information that they are looking for in the personal statement. This chapter will guide you on what you should say and how you should say it.

Why physiotherapy?

A high proportion of UCAS applications contain the sentence: 'From an early age I have wanted to be a physiotherapist because it is the only career that combines my love of science with the chance to work with people.' Not only do admissions tutors get bored with reading this, but it is also clearly untrue; if you think about it, there are many careers that combine science and people, including teaching, pharmacy, dentistry and nursing. However, the basic ideas behind this sentence may well apply to you.

If so, you need to personalise it. You could mention an incident that first got you interested in physiotherapy – a visit to a physiotherapist, a conversation with a family friend or a lecture at school, for instance. You could write about your interest in human biology, or about a biology project that you undertook when you were younger, to illustrate your interest in science, and you could give examples of how you like to work with others. The important thing is to back up your initial interest in physiotherapy with your efforts to investigate the career.

What have you done to investigate physiotherapy?

This is the one part that cannot be stressed highly enough. This is where you describe your work experience. It is important to demonstrate that you gained something from the work experience, and that it has given you an insight into the profession. You should give an indication of the length of time that you spent at each work placement, what treatments you observed, and your impressions of physiotherapy.

You could comment on what aspects of physiotherapy attract you, what you found interesting, or something that surprised you. It is not enough to give details of where you worked and what you saw: the selectors will be asking themselves what you learnt from the experience. Here is an example of a description of a student's work experience that would not have impressed the selectors.

> I spent three days at my local hospital's physiotherapy ward. I saw some patients having ultrasounds, and a man who went in the hydrotherapy pool. It was very interesting.

The next example would have been much more convincing because it is clear that the student was interested in what was happening.

> During my three weeks at Melchester General Hospital I was able to shadow two physiotherapists. I watched a range of treatments including ultrasound and exercise in the hydrotherapy pool. I was particularly interested in the ultrasound treatment because I had only ever seen it used for diagnosis. In the cases that I saw during my work experience it was used to stimulate healing in muscle tissue that had been damaged in an accident. Most of the patients that I saw receiving treatment were elderly. I was able to spend some time with a man who had suffered a stroke and had limited use of his hands. The physiotherapist worked with him on a series of repetitive exercises to try to get him to be able to perform simple tasks. I was also able to see the importance of teamwork because the physio-therapist worked alongside a speech therapist as the man had also lost the ability to communicate effectively.

With luck, the selectors may pick up on this at interview and ask ques-tions about the methods that the physiotherapists used; the student could then bring in his or her knowledge of ultrasound (having investi-gated it following the work experience). This student would also have gained extra credit with the admissions tutors for having arranged lengthier work experience placements.

Personal qualities

As a physiotherapist you will be working with others throughout your career. To qualify as a physiotherapist you will study alongside maybe 30 others in your year, for three years.

To be a successful physiotherapist you need to be able to relate to other people; to survive and enjoy university you need to be able to get on with a wide range of people too. Unlike school life, where many of the activities are organised and arranged by the teachers, almost all of the social activities at university are instigated and organised by the students. For this reason the selectors are looking for people who have the enthusiasm and ability to motivate others, and are prepared to give up their own time to arrange sporting, dramatic, musical or social activities.

Extracurricular activities

How, then, does the person reading your personal statement know whether you have the qualities that they are looking for? They will expect to read about some of the following:

- participation in team events
- involvement in school plays or concerts
- positions of responsibility
- work in the local community
- part-time or holiday jobs
- charity work.

The selectors will be aware that some schools offer more in the way of activities and responsibilities than others, and they will make allowances for this. You do not have to have been on a school expedition to India or to be head girl to be considered, but you need to be able to demonstrate that you have taken the best possible advantage of what is on offer. The selectors will be aware of the type of school or college that you have come from (there is a box on the back of the UCAS application that your referee fills in) and, consequently, the opportunities that are open to you. What they are looking for is that you have grasped these opportunities.

General tips

- Do not attempt to copy passages from other sources and incorporate them in your personal statement. UCAS uses anti-plagiarism software when checking statements; if you have used material from someone else (including the examples in this book), you will be caught out and your application will be void.

- Do not be tempted to get someone else (a friend, teacher, parent or one of the many internet sites that offer 'help') to write your personal statement. It has to sound like you, which is why it is called a personal statement.

- Although you can apply for up to five institutions or courses, you write only one personal statement, and so it needs to be relevant to all of the courses you are applying for. You will not be able to write a convincing statement if you are applying to a variety of different courses.

- Print off a copy of your personal statement so that you can remind yourself of all the wonderful things you said, should you be called for interview!

- If you are planning to do so, state your reasons for applying for deferred entry and outline what you intend to do during your gap year. For example, you might be planning to find some relevant work experience in a firm of solicitors, and then spend some time overseas to brush up your language skills.

- Do not be tempted to use overly formal or long-winded English.

- Read through a draft of your statement, and ask yourself the question: 'Does it sound like me?' If not, rewrite it.

- Avoid phrases such as 'I was fortunate enough to be able to shadow a physiotherapist ...' when you really mean 'I shadowed a physiotherapist ...' or 'I arranged to shadow a physiotherapist ...'

A sample personal statement

I first became interested in becoming a physiotherapist following treatment for a knee injury. This interest was confirmed after attending a seminar given to our school science society on biomechanics, and by undertaking several work experience placements. In my local hospital I worked alongside physiotherapists on a neurological rehabilitation ward and was able to observe hydrotherapy treatment and also the treatment of children with cystic fibrosis. I have been helping with a wide range of exercise programmes both in and out of the hydrotherapy pool, and have benefited from the training on subjects that are relevant to children. I have also been involved in teaching swimming to children with learning disabilities and visiting elderly people. This range of experience has helped me to understand the differing demands placed on therapists, the importance of mutual trust and teamwork, and the place of physiotherapy within healthcare.

I have a part-time job in my local supermarket dealing with customer enquiries. I found this stressful at first because almost everyone I had to deal with wanted to complain about something! But I soon learnt how to calm them down and to help them to sort out their problems by remaining calm and polite and by listening to what they had to say. I think that this has helped me in my voluntary work as well. I chose Physics and Sociology at A level, alongside Biology, because they will help me when I study physiotherapy at university. Physics helps me to develop my problem-solving skills as well as my understanding of the mechanics of movement; and sociology deals with important issues such as health and illness.

I participate in many sports, am captain of the school 1st VII netball team and have also played for the 1st XI hockey team. I enjoy textiles and have made several rugs and items of clothing. I like photography, particularly the work of Ansel Adams, who photographed landscapes, and his work has inspired me to go to a number of national parks to take pictures. I go to the cinema and theatre as often as I can and I like music. I have taken grade 7 clarinet and am learning the guitar, which I play badly in a band that I formed with some friends. We have yet to play in public! For my gap year I have arranged to spend six months working in a school for children with serious physical disabilities, and I will then travel with friends to India, Thailand and Vietnam.

5 | At full stretch
The interview

If the selectors like the picture that the UCAS application has painted of you they will call you for interview. The purpose of the interview is to allow them to see whether this picture is an accurate one, and to investigate whether you have a genuine interest in physiotherapy. You must be aware of current events in the profession; this is discussed in Chapter 6. The interviewers will generally ask you three types of question:

1. those designed to relax you so that they can assess your communication skills
2. those designed to investigate your interest and suitability for physiotherapy
3. those designed to get a clearer picture of your personal qualities.

Questions to get you relaxed

'How was your journey here today?'

The interviewers are not really interested in the details of your travel. Do not be tempted to give them a minute-by-minute account of your bus journey ('. . . and then we waited for six minutes at the road works on Corporation Street . . .'), but also do not simply say 'OK'. Say something like: 'It was fine, thank you. The train journey took about two hours, which gave me the chance to catch up on some reading.' With a bit of luck they will ask you what you read, which gives you the chance to talk about a book, newspaper article or an item in *Frontline*.

'I am interested to know why you decided to apply to Melchester.'

Another variation on this might be: 'How did you narrow your choice down to five universities?' The panel will be looking for evidence of research, and that your reasons are based on informed judgement.

Probably the best possible answer would start with 'I came to your open day . . .' because you can then proceed to tell them why you like their university so much, what impressed you about the course and facilities and how the atmosphere of the place would particularly suit you. Even if you are unable to attend open days, try to arrange a formal or informal visit before you are interviewed so that you can show that you are aware of the environment, both academic and physical, and that you like the place. If you know people who are at the university or on the course, so much the better.

You should also know about the course structure. On pages 15–16 there is an overview of the differences and similarities between courses, and the prospectus will give detailed information. Given the choice between a candidate who is not only going to make a good physiotherapist, but clearly wants to come to their institution, and another who may have the right qualities but does not seem to care whether he or she studies there or somewhere else, whom do you think the selectors will choose?

Answers to avoid include the following:

- 'Reputation' (unless you know in detail the areas for which the university is highly regarded).
- 'It's in London, and I don't want to move away from my friends.'
- 'You take a lot of retake students.'
- 'My dad says it is easy to get a place here.'

A good answer could be: 'I came to an open day last summer, which is why I have applied here. I enjoyed the day, and was impressed by the facilities, and by the comments of the students who showed us around because they seemed so enthusiastic about the course. Also, my cousin studied English at the university and I visited her, and got to sample the atmosphere of the town.'

There are variations on this question. The interviewers may ask you what you know about the course, or about the university. In all cases this is your chance to show the interviewers that you are desperate to come to their university.

> **WARNING!**
>
> Do your homework by reading the prospectus and looking at the website. Although on the surface all physiotherapy courses appear to cover broadly the same subjects, there are big differences in how the courses are delivered and in the opportunities for patient contact, and your interviewers will expect you to know about their course.

Questions about physiotherapy

'Why do you want to be a physiotherapist?'

This is the question that all interviewees expect. Given that the interviewers will be aware that you are expecting the question, they will also expect your answer to be planned carefully. If you look surprised, and say something like 'Um . . . well . . . I haven't really thought about why . . .' you can expect to be rejected. Other answers to avoid are: 'The money'; 'I couldn't get into medicine'; 'I want to help people'; 'I want to work for Arsenal'.

Many students are worried that they will sound insincere when they answer this question. The way to avoid this is to try to bring in reasons that are personal to you, for instance an incident that started your interest (perhaps a visit to a physiotherapist), or an aspect of your work experience that particularly fascinated you. The important thing is to try to express clearly what interested you rather than try to generalise your answers. Rather than say 'Physiotherapy combines science, working with people and the chance to have control over your career', which says little about you, tell the interviewers about the way in which your interest progressed. Here is an example of a good answer.

Although it seemed strange to my friends, I used to enjoy going with my grandfather to a physiotherapist when he had difficulty in walking due to arthritis. This was because the physiotherapist explained things very clearly and patiently, and I was interested in what was happening around me. My favourite subject is biology, particularly the anatomy side of it, and I always wanted to do something that involved this. When I was thinking about my career I arranged to shadow another physiotherapist, and the more time I spent at the hospital the more I realised that this would really suit me. This also gave me the chance to find out about what being a physiotherapist is really like. The things about physiotherapy that I particularly enjoy are . . .'

WARNING!

Do not learn this passage and repeat it at your interview. Ensure that your answer is not only personal to you, but also honest.

With luck, the interviewers will pick up on something that you said about work experience and ask you more questions about this. Since 'Why do you want to be a physiotherapist?' is such an obvious question, interviewers often try to find out the information in different ways. Expect questions such as 'When did your interest in physiotherapy start?', 'What was it about your work experience that finally convinced you that physiotherapy was for you?' or 'I see that you spent two weeks with your physiotherapist. Was there anything that surprised you?'

Variations on this question could include 'Was there anything that particularly interested you?', 'Was there anything you found off-putting?' or simply 'Tell me about your work experience'. What these questions really mean is: 'Are you able to show us that you were interested in what was happening during your work experience?' Returning to the original question, answering either 'Yes' or 'No' without explanation will not gain you many marks. Similarly, saying 'Yes, I was surprised by the number of patients who seemed very scared' says nothing about your awareness of the physiotherapist's approach to his or her patients.

However, answering 'Yes, I was surprised by the number of patients who seemed very scared. What struck me, however, was the way in which the physiotherapist dealt with each patient as an individual, sometimes being sympathetic, sometimes explaining things in great detail and sometimes using humour to relax them. For instance . . .' shows that you were interested enough to be aware of more than the most obvious things.

Sentences that start with 'For example . . .' and 'For instance . . .' are particularly important as they allow you to demonstrate your interest. In order to be able to give examples, you should keep a diary of things that you saw during your work experience so that you do not forget. You should read through this before your interview, as if you were revising for an examination.

'I see that you try to keep up to date with developments in physiotherapy. Can you tell me about something that you have read about recently?'

If you are interested in making physiotherapy your career, the selectors will expect you to be interested enough in the subject to want to read about it. Good sources of information are the CSP's website and others (addresses are given in Chapter 10), *Frontline* and the national newspapers. You should get into the habit of looking at a broadsheet newspaper every day to see if there are any medical or physiotherapy-related stories.

Note that the question uses the word 'recently': recent does not mean an article you read two years ago – keep up to date. You could, for instance, say: 'There was a recent report that sportspeople risk injury from air-filled training shoes. There was a survey of basketball players which showed that they were four times more likely to suffer ankle injuries if they were wearing trainers with soles that contained air pockets.'

'During your work experience, you had the chance to discuss physiotherapy with physiotherapists. What do you know about career opportunities and pay for physiotherapists?'

You must make sure that you do some research on career paths by asking questions about this when you meet physiotherapists.

Most physiotherapists work in the NHS, but there are many other options. On pages 8–9 we described many of the types of work undertaken by physiotherapists. Most physiotherapists end up specialising in one or more particular areas – in most cases as a result of an interest that grew during their training. The best answer to a question like this is to describe the career paths of physiotherapists you have met and worked with, as this will allow you to highlight your own work experience.

'What qualities should a physiotherapist possess?'

These have been discussed on page 36. However, do not simply list them. The question has not been asked because the interviewer is puzzled about what these qualities are; it has been asked to give you a chance to show:

- that you are aware of them, and
- that you possess them.

The best way to answer this is to use phrases such as 'During my work experience at the Melchester Physiotherapy Clinic I was able to observe/talk to the physiotherapist, and I became aware that . . .', or 'Communication is very important. For instance, when I was shadowing my physiotherapist, there was a patient who . . .' Try always to relate these general questions to your own experiences.

'Physiotherapy requires high levels of physical fitness and manual dexterity. Do you possess these?'

Manual manipulation of a patient's limbs requires a fair degree of fitness and strength, and as a physiotherapist you will need to be able to help to lift and lower patients. If you have trouble picking up a coffee cup without breathing heavily for the next 10 minutes, physiotherapy may not be the best career for you. The interviewers will need to be reassured that you are able to work in a physically demanding environment, and also that you have the manual dexterity necessary to perform sometimes intricate tasks. Try to anticipate this question by preparing an answer which demonstrates that you have these qualities. Sport is always a good indicator of fitness and coordination, but you could also mention situations that you encountered during your work experience, demanding tasks that you perform as part of a weekend job, expeditions that you have been on at school as part of the Duke of Edinburgh's Award, or a hobby such as DIY.

> **WARNING!**
>
> Do not lie about the example you describe. An admissions tutor I talked to recounted the story of an applicant who wrote in the UCAS application that he worked for a local Riding for the Disabled scheme. However, the previous interview had been with someone from the same town who had explained that there was no such scheme in the area, which is why she could not carry on doing this when she moved there. He was found out, and rejected.

Questions to find out about what sort of person you are

'What do you do to relax?'

Do not say 'watch TV' or 'go to the pub'. Mention something that involves working or communicating with others, for instance sport or music. Use the question to demonstrate that you possess the qualities required in a physiotherapist. However, do not make your answer so insincere that the interviewers realise that you are trying to impress them. Saying 'I relax most effectively when I go to the local physiotherapy clinic to shadow the physiotherapist' will not convince them.

'How do you cope with stress?'

Physiotherapy can be a stressful occupation. Physiotherapists have to deal with difficult people, those who are scared and those who react badly when in a physiotherapy ward. For many people, physiotherapy can be painful and distressing and patients are not always cooperative, or even aware of why they are receiving treatment. In these circumstances the physiotherapist cannot panic, but must remain calm and rational. The interviewers will want to make a judgement as to whether you will be able to cope with the demands of the job.

Having been through them themselves, it is unlikely that they will regard school examinations as being particularly stressful. Hard work, yes, but not as stressful as training to be a physiotherapist or practising as a physiotherapist. What they are looking for are answers that demonstrate your calmness and composure when dealing with others. You could relate it to your work experience, or your Saturday job. Dealing with a queue of angry and impatient customers demanding to know why their cheeseburgers are not ready can be difficult. Other areas that can provide evidence of stress management are school expeditions, public speaking or positions of responsibility at school or outside.

'I see that you enjoy reading. What is the most recent book that you have read?'

The question might be about the cinema or theatre, but the point of it is the same: to get you talking about something that interests you. Although it may sound obvious, if you have written that you enjoy reading in your UCAS application make sure that you have actually read something recently. Admissions tutors will be able to tell you stories about interviewees who look at them with absolute amazement when they are asked about books, despite it featuring in the personal statement. Answers such as 'Well . . . I haven't had much time recently, but . . . let me see . . . I read *Elle* last month, and . . . oh yes . . . I had to read *Jane Eyre* for my English GCSE' will do your chances no good at all. By all means put down that you like reading, but make sure that you have read an interesting novel in the period leading up to the interview, and be prepared to discuss it.

How to succeed in your interview

You should prepare for an interview as if you are preparing for an examination. This involves revision of your work experience diary so that you can recount details of your time with physiotherapists, revision of the newspaper, website and *Frontline* articles that you have saved, and revision of all of the things that you have mentioned on your personal statement.

> *'My interviews concentrated on my work experience. They really probed me about what being a physiotherapist is really like – not just what I did, but what it is like working as a physiotherapist day in and day out, so I'm glad I did it.'*
>
> Adam, Nottingham University

When you are preparing for your A levels you sit a mock examination so that the real thing does not come as a total surprise; when you are preparing for an interview have a mock interview so that you can get some feedback on your answers. Your school may be able to help you. If not, independent sixth-form colleges usually provide a mock interview service. Friends of your parents may also be able to help. If possible, video your mock interview so that you are aware of the way you come across in an interview situation. There is a list of practice interview questions below.

Mock interview questions

- Why do you want to be a physiotherapist?
- What have you done to investigate physiotherapy?

- Why does physiotherapy interest you more than medicine/nursing/radiography?
- What are the ideal qualities that a physiotherapist should possess?
- Do you possess these qualities?
- Give me an example of how you cope with stress.
- Why did you apply to this university?
- Did you come to our open day?
- During your work experience, did anything surprise you?
- During your work experience, did anything shock you?
- Was the physiotherapist you shadowed good at communicating with his/her patients?
- Tell me about preventive physiotherapy.
- What is occupational therapy?
- What is repetitive strain injury?
- What is cystic fibrosis/a stroke/arthritis?
- What is hydrotherapy?
- What is ultrasound and how is it used?
- Is exercise always good for you?
- How much do NHS physiotherapists earn?
- Have you read any articles about physiotherapy recently?
- What advances can we expect in physiotherapy technology/treatment in the future?
- What have you done to demonstrate your commitment to the community?
- What would you contribute to this university?
- What are your best/worst qualities?
- What was the last novel you read? What did you think of it?
- What was the last play/film you saw? What did you think of it?
- What do you do to relax?
- What is your favourite A level subject?
- What grades do you expect to gain in your A levels?
- What precautions need to be taken with patients who are HIV positive?
- How does teamwork apply to the role of a physiotherapist?
- What branch of physiotherapy interests you the most, and why?
- What is the role of a physiotherapist in a hospital?
- Why are communication skills important for physiotherapists?
- What have you done that demonstrates your communication skills?
- What have you done that demonstrates your leadership skills?
- What have you done that demonstrates your ability to cope in a stressful situation?
- Why is a knowledge of physics helpful in physiotherapy?
- What are the particular difficulties that animal physiotherapists encounter?
- How did you organise your work experience?
- Why are you taking a gap year?

Appearance and body language

Appearance and body language are important. The impression you create can be very influential. Remember that if the interviewers cannot picture you as a physiotherapist in future years they are unlikely to offer you a place.

Body language

- Maintain eye contact with the interviewers.
- Direct most of what you are saying to the person who asked you the question, but occasionally look around at the others on the panel.
- Sit up straight, but adopt a position that you feel comfortable in.
- Do not wave your hands around too much, but do not keep them gripped together to stop them moving. Fold them across your lap, or rest them on the arms of the chair.

Speech

- Talk slowly and clearly.
- Do not use slang.
- Avoid saying 'erm . . .', 'you know' or 'sort of'.
- Say 'hello' at the start of the interview, and 'thank you' and 'good-bye' at the end.

Dress and appearance

- Wear clothes that show you have made an effort for the interview.
- You do not have to wear a business suit, but a jacket and tie (men) or a skirt and blouse (women) are appropriate.
- Make sure that you are clean and tidy.
- If appropriate, shave before the interview (but avoid overpowering aftershave).
- Clean your nails and shoes.
- Wash your hair.
- Avoid (visible) piercings, earrings (men), jeans and trainers.

At the end of the interview

You may be given the opportunity to ask a question at the end of the interview. Bear in mind that the interviews are carefully timed, and that your attempts to impress the panel with 'clever' questions may do quite the opposite. The golden rule is: only ask a question if you are genuinely interested in the answer (which, of course, you were unable to find during your careful reading of the prospectus).

Questions to avoid

- What is the structure of the first year of the course?
- Will I be able to live in a hall of residence?
- When will I first have contact with patients?

As well as being boring questions, the answers to these will be available in the prospectus. You have obviously not done any serious research.

Questions you could ask

- 'I haven't studied physics at AS level. Should I go through some physics textbooks before the start of the course?' This shows that you are keen, and that you want to make sure that you can cope with the course. It will give the selectors a chance to talk about the extra course they offer for non-physicists.
- 'Do you think I should try to get more work experience before the start of the course?' Again, an indication of your keenness.
- 'Earlier, I couldn't answer the question you asked me on ultrasound. What is the answer?' Something that you genuinely might want to know.
- 'How soon will you let me know if I have been successful or not?' Something you really want to know.

REMEMBER!

If in doubt, do not ask a question. End by saying 'All of my questions have been answered by the prospectus and the students who showed me around the university. Thank you very much for an interesting day.' Smile, shake hands (if appropriate – if you are being interviewed by a panel of five, who are all sitting at the other end of a long table, then do not!) and say goodbye.

Structuring the interview

The selectors will have a set of questions that they may ask, designed to assess your suitability and commitment. If you answer 'Yes' or 'No' to most questions, or reply only in monosyllables, they will fire more and more questions at you. If, however, your answers are longer and also contain statements that interest them, they are more likely to pick up on these, and you are, effectively, directing the interview. If you are asked questions that you have prepared for there will be less time for the interviewers to ask you questions that might be more difficult to answer.

For example, at the end of your answer to a question about work experience, you might say '. . . and the physiotherapist was able to explain the effect of new technology on physiotherapy.' The interviewer may then say: 'I see. Can you tell me about how technology is changing physiotherapy?' You can then embark on an answer about ultrasound, for instance. At the end of your explanation you could finish with: '. . . of course, ultrasound treatment is often used in conjunction with infrared radiation treatment.' You may then be asked about situations where this might happen, and so on.

Of course, this does not always work, but you would be very unlucky not to have at least one of these 'signposts' that you placed in front of them followed.

How you are selected

During the interview the panel will be assessing you in various categories. Whether or not the interview appears to be structured, the interviewers will be following careful guidelines so that they can compare candidates from different interview sessions. Some panels adopt a conversational style, whereas others are more formal. The scoring system will vary from place to place but, in general, you will be assessed in the following categories:

● reason for your choice of university
● academic ability
● motivation for physiotherapy
● awareness of physiotherapy issues
● personal qualities
● communication skills.

You are likely to be scored in each category, and the university will have a minimum mark that you will have to gain if you are to be made an offer. If you are below this score, but close to it, you may be put on an official or unofficial waiting list. If this happens you may be considered in August, should there be places available.

If you are offered a place you will receive a letter from the university telling you what you need to achieve in your A levels. This is called a conditional offer. Post-A level students who have achieved the necessary grades will be given unconditional offers. If you are unlucky, all you will get is an email from UCAS saying that you have been rejected. If this happens it is not necessarily the end of the road that leads you to a career in physiotherapy.

If you are rejected by all of your choices, you can enter the UCAS Extra scheme which allows you to contact other universities. If you still are without a place when the A level results are released in August, you are eligible to apply for vacant places through Clearing.

When UCAS has received replies from all of your choices they will send you a Statement of Offers. You will then have about a month to make up your mind about where you want to go. If you have only one offer you have little choice but to accept it. If you have more than one you have to accept one as your firm choice, and another (usually a lower offer) as your insurance choice. If the place where you really want to study makes a lower offer than one of your other choices, do not be tempted to choose the lower offer as your insurance choice, since you are obliged to go to the university that you have put as your firm choice if you achieve the grades. Even if you narrowly miss you may still be accepted by your first choice. If you decide that you do not want to go there, once the results are issued, you will have to withdraw from the UCAS system for that year.

6 | Do you know your gluteus maximus from your articulatio cubiti?
Current issues

This chapter explains the most relevant current issues in physiotherapy. This should be used as a reference point for your interview but not the only source of your information. You should make sure that you read newspapers and journals (such as *Frontline*) to get ideas on other current issues and not just rely on those listed here. Your success at interview will depend on your ability to converse fluently on up-to-date topics. You do not have to be an expert in your field – that is what they are – but you do need to have tried to understand the profession that you wish to follow. If that comes as a surprise to you, this is not the right career!

Technology in physiotherapy

Enter the words 'physiotherapy' and 'news' into an internet search engine and most of the links that you get are to news stories about new forms of treatment. Although the basic techniques used in physiotherapy have been around for a long time – physical manipulation, repetition of exercises and other forms of manual therapy – technology plays an increasingly important role.

Probably the most widely used application of technology within physiotherapy is ultrasound. Ultrasound treatment utilises high-frequency (up to 3MHz – too high for the human ear to hear) sound waves. Ultrasound is used extensively in medicine for diagnosis, either to form images in order to see what is happening inside the body (for instance, scans that show a foetus inside the womb) or to measure blood flow.

Whenever ultrasound waves pass from one tissue to another, a small percentage of the beam is reflected back, and these reflected sound waves are used to create a picture, or to measure the speed at which blood is flowing (using something called the Doppler effect). Ultrasound can also be used therapeutically; that is, for treatment. It has been used to accelerate tissue repair and to relieve pain since the 1950s. It is used to treat a variety of conditions such as sports injuries, sprains, tendonitis, arthritis and ulcers, and to relieve the pain associated with, for instance, phantom limbs in amputees. The sound waves penetrate deep into the body and, although the biological effects are not completely understood, it is likely that the vibration caused by the sound waves produces a combination of heating (thermal effects) and stimulation of tissue and blood vessels (mechanical effects). Ultrasound is usually given at the end of a course of treatment, following other forms of manual therapy.

Ultrasound equipment is relatively cheap to buy (less than £2,000 for an ultrasound machine) and is easy to use. The total cost to the NHS of ultrasound in physiotherapy is around £5 million per year – a tiny proportion of the total NHS bill. The drawbacks of the extensive use of ultrasound in physiotherapy are that there is little conclusive clinical evidence that it is effective and that there is a possible risk of tissue damage if the power settings on individual machines are not calibrated accurately.

Another treatment that utilises sound waves, extracorporeal shockwave therapy (ESWT), has been introduced into physiotherapy clinics. ESWT was brought to a wider audience in 2004 when Sachin Tendulkar, the Indian cricketer, received shockwave therapy to treat tennis elbow that had failed to respond to conventional physiotherapy. Developed from the devices that generate pulses of sound waves to destroy kidney stones, ESWT devices produce pulses of high-pressure sound that travel through the skin. Soft tissue and bone that are subjected to these pulses of high-pressure energy heal back stronger. Tennis elbow results from calcification of a tendon and is usually treated with mechanical exercise or steroid injection (which risk weakening the tendon still further), but new treatments are also being developed.

There are instances of robots being used in physiotherapy. This does not mean that next time you require physiotherapy you will be treated by R2-D2, Bender or Kryton. The effective rehabilitation of patients with cerebral palsy, or following a stroke or other brain injuries, requires repetitive movement exercises and controllable resistance to motion. In one such treatment the patient is coupled to a robot joystick that guides him or her through a series of movements. The robot can be programmed to vary the scope of the movement, to increase or decrease the resistance, or to help the patient to complete the movements. To increase interest levels for the patient, the movements can be integrated into a 'game' on a screen in front of the patient. In this way tens of thousands of therapeutic movements can be completed over the course of a few weeks – far more than the physiotherapist could manage, and more than the patient is likely to be able to accomplish alone. Virtual reality is also used to alleviate the boredom often associated with repetitive exercises. Patients can put themselves into a virtual reality environment where they can take part in a game that requires them to perform the necessary therapeutic movements.

Obesity

Obesity is one of the biggest health challenges that we face in this country. This is an issue that the government is now actively trying to combat, as one in four adults in England is currently obese. The statistics from the Department of Health show that if the trend continues in this way, then by 2050, nine in 10 adults will be overweight. The cost to the NHS is roughly £4.2 billion (estimated to be £6.3 billion by 2015) and £16 billion to the wider economy.

As we have discussed previously, prevention is just as important as cure. Working alongside other schemes such as the healthy eating Change4Life movement, the CSP is currently targeting this issue with the Move for Health campaign, which encourages the public to take control of their health and wellbeing by taking part in regular exercise. The recommendation from the CSP is that an adult exercises five times a week at moderate intensity for roughly 30 minutes. If that is not physically possible, i.e. you have time constraints that do not allow a concentrated period of exercise, then manage your time effectively and split the 30 minutes into shorter sessions at different intervals throughout the day. It may sound obvious, but this will have a positive effect on your health if continued over a long period of time.

The campaign is designed to show people that increased levels of physical activity can prevent, or help to control, in excess of 20 medical conditions, most notably obesity, osteoarthritis, heart disease, type 2 diabetes and other conditions affecting wellbeing such as depression. If nothing else, releasing endorphins through increased levels of activity will have a positive effect on productivity and output during a working day. It is a complete endorsement of the adage 'healthy body, healthy mind'.

Childhood obesity

This issue is particularly important in terms of preventing our children from becoming obese and protecting future generations. In order to address the dangers that obesity can have on children's health, a scheme similar to its older sibling is being run by the CSP. Working alongside the British Dietetic Association, the Move for Health Kids campaign gives the recommendation that children should exercise for at least an hour every day. Would you have known that Jamie Oliver and physiotherapists are so hand in hand?

Parkinson's disease

The international guidelines for physiotherapists who treat patients with Parkinson's disease have now been adapted for use in the UK.

Following the research and evidence-based work that was done by the Royal Dutch Society for Physical Therapy, the Parkinson's Disease Society put in a place a project to make these guidelines accessible for clinical use in this country. One of the main innovative features of these guidelines is that they include four 'quick reference' cards to be used in clinical practice, whether that be in clinics, on wards or in the community.

These guidelines are an update of those published by the National Institute for Health and Clinical Excellence in 2006. Those working in the profession have argued that they are more applicable as they focus on the areas that affect the physiotherapist, such as assessment, treatment and outcome measurement, as opposed to the strictly medicine-based approach of their peers.

Repetitive strain injury

Repetitive strain injury (RSI) is an increasingly common complaint among computer users. As the name suggests, the condition is caused by repetition of certain movements, usually associated with computer keyboard use. However, it is not confined to computer users and has been diagnosed in many people whose jobs involve manual labour or machine operation. The condition can also occur when the person's posture is inappropriate to the task that he or she is undertaking.

RSI manifests itself as pain, mostly when the task that caused it is being carried out, but often at other times as well. It usually affects the neck, shoulders, elbows, wrists or hands. RSI is also known by other names including WRMSD (work-related musculoskeletal disorder), WRULD (work-related upper limb disorder), CTD (cumulative trauma disorder) and OOS (occupational overuse syndrome). The term RSI actually encompasses a number of different conditions, most commonly carpal tunnel syndrome. 'Carpal' comes from the Greek word *karpos*, which means wrist. The joint in the wrist is surrounded by fibrous tissue, and there is a small gap between this tissue and the bone, through which a nerve (the median nerve) passes. The nerve then splits to serve the fingers and thumb. Repetitive movement of the wrist can cause swelling of the tissue in the wrist, putting pressure on the median nerve. Symptoms include numbness and tingling in the fingers and thumb, followed by pain. The condition can usually be cured by a combination of physiotherapy and rest.

People who work in factories are three times more likely to get RSI than office workers, reports the CSP. They say: 'Over 370,000 people in Great Britain are afflicted with RSI and as many as 86,000 new cases were recorded last year. In terms of employee absence, lower productivity and staff turnover, the cost to employers is nearly £300 million!'

The CSP website reports that the Labour Research Department analysed Health and Safety Executive figures for the CSP and discovered that metal, plastics, textile and other plant and machine workers were the most likely to get RSI (1.1 per 100 workers), followed by bricklayers, plumbers, carpenters and others in skilled trades (0.91 per 100 workers). Professionals (0.32) and managers (0.36) were the least likely to get RSI.

Not everyone believes that RSI actually exists. Carpal tunnel syndrome certainly does and can be caused by obesity, arthritis, diabetes and pregnancy, but there are those who are sceptical as to whether repetitive movement is a cause. A report in the British Medical Journal on research done at Manchester University cast some doubts about RSI. The research indicated that the majority of those who suffered from arm or wrist pain (105 people in a survey encompassing 1,200 volunteers) were also the most dissatisfied with their jobs and suffered from high stress levels. In other words, the pain could be due to psychological or stress factors rather than simply the physical aspects of their jobs.

Rehabilitation of stroke patients

A stroke occurs when a blood clot blocks a blood vessel in the brain, causing brain cells in the area to die. If treatment is not given immediately, further cells in the surrounding areas also die. The functions such as speech, memory or movement that were controlled by these brain cells are then affected, depending on the area of the brain where the blood vessels were blocked. The severity of the stroke can vary from patient to patient, and the effects may be very minor (and temporary) or they may lead to paralysis or death.

The main types of rehabilitation are:

- **physical therapy–** to improve mechanical skills such as walking, use of the hands, or balance
- **occupational therapy** – to re-learn the skills that are required for everyday life such as eating, dressing and looking after oneself
- **speech therapy** – to re-learn how to communicate effectively.

Physiotherapy for stroke patients must begin as early as possible following the stroke in order to be effective. Improvement is slow and recovery is difficult six months after the stroke. However, paralysed muscles must not be treated too early or they may be damaged permanently. Research carried out at the University of Texas, reported in *New*

Scientist, found that rats and monkeys that had received small brain injuries to cause paralysis of a limb suffered further injury if treatment was started immediately. The researchers surmised that glutamate, a neurotransmitter that is released during movement, was the probable cause, since, in large concentrations, it acts as a toxin. Brain damage appeared to multiply its effects. Research is now being carried out to find drugs that will block the effects of glutamate.

The expertise of the physiotherapist is vital in assessing when (and in what form) treatment should start. At the start of the treatment, the physiotherapist will prepare muscles for the more intensive treatments that will follow, and will work on enabling the patient to support his or her own weight if leg muscles are affected. The later stages of physiotherapy may involve compensation for permanently damaged muscles through the introduction of aids such as walking frames. The physiotherapist may work alongside occupational therapists, speech therapists, carers and psychologists to try to prepare the patient for a return to 'normal' life.

Exercise referral schemes

Introduced 18 years ago, NHS exercise referral schemes have become increasingly popular. In 2004 the government outlined proposals to provide GPs with national standards for 'prescribing' exercise programmes for their patients.

Exercise referral schemes are used to help patients suffering from a wide range of problems, including:

- coronary heart disease
- diabetes
- hypertension
- mental health problems, including depression
- musculoskeletal problems, e.g. chronic low-back pain
- obesity
- problems caused by falls.

In the 10-year review in July 2004, the CSP published figures showing that the number of schemes had mushroomed by over 500% during the previous decade. In 1994, there were 157 exercise referral schemes in existence, compared with the latest estimate of 816. The Chief Executive of the CSP, quoted on the CSP website, said: 'This report highlights the way in which exercise referral schemes are of particular benefit to patients at risk of heart attack and stroke. They are also helping people successfully tackle obesity, diabetes, mental health problems and low-back pain. However, various sources in November 2011 reported that much uncertainty remains over the effectiveness of such schemes for increasing physical activity, as a result of a meta-analysis of other studies. Physiotherapists play crucial roles in the prevention and management of these conditions and are ideally placed to help roll out a wider network of schemes.'

Andrée Deane, Executive Chair of the Fitness Industry Association at the time, welcomed the initiative: 'Exercise referral schemes provide great opportunities for fitness professionals to work in partnership with health professionals on schemes that target people who do not normally take exercise. These can make a real contribution to public health.'

NHS reform 2011

Andrew Lansley (Secretary of State for Health) released the White Paper on health reform *Equity and excellence: Liberating the NHS* in July 2010 for implementation in 2011. (For more on this White Paper go to www.bma.org.uk/healthcare_policy/nhs_white_paper/gpcwhite-paperguidance.jsp.)

The main point of the reform was to revert power back to the patients and their carers and put them in charge of making decisions about their health and wellbeing. As a result, 2011 was a defining year for the NHS. The health service face the biggest shake-up since its foundation. Andrew Lansley believed this would be achieved by devolving an £80 billion budget to around 500 GP consortiums, which in turn would buy services such as operations or scans from hospitals and other specialists. The consortiums would be able to choose who to buy the services from, possibly even from outside the UK. The 151 primary healthcare trusts would be phased out. The aim is to save the NHS £5 billion (not forgetting that the scheme will cost £1.4 billion to set up) and the changes are to be implemented fully by 2013.

Impact on physiotherapy

After a decade of yearly budget rises under the previous Labour government, the NHS is to reduce its services with a £20 billion 'efficiency savings' drive. This is most notable in services in England. Cuts to services were announced in 2011 amid claims from the coalition government that frontline care would be protected. This means that those with chronic illnesses have had NHS physiotherapy services cut. Specifically, priority 2 and 3 cases either have had sessions removed altogether or have had their sessions reduced by two-thirds. In some cases, those in need of physiotherapy are facing waits of up to six months, which is sometimes too long.

Injuries such as back problems or arthritis in the knee have seen physiotherapy treatment removed; the focus is now on briefly educating patients on their treatment and giving advice on stretching. The CSP revealed that out of 1,000 members, 74% had seen a rationing of quality services. Some 87% were concerned about the result this was having on the number of sessions a patient would have; 81% were concerned about long waiting times; and 71% thought that some people's conditions could become chronic as a result of delays and denial of treatment or lead to re-admittance to hospital. Also of concern are those 250,000 people in Britain with severe asthma who face waiting times of up to six months on average. This affects not only direct patient care but also the teaching of parents in how to help their children, particularly those suffering from breathing difficulties. With the cuts, there is no time to allow for this.

CSP members are concerned that patient care will suffer under the government's reforms. CSP Chief Executive Phil Gray said: 'Physiotherapists are concerned that this reorganisation, which is unprecedented in size and scale, will have devastating consequences for patients.' He also went on to say that the budget cuts meant that: 'Patients are facing longer waiting times, fewer sessions with a physiotherapist and, in the most extreme cases, could get no treatment whatsoever.'

Phil Gray told the *Observer*: 'In order to save money, some patients will only receive advice . . . That is quite simply a scandal.'

His words are backed up by charities such as Asthma UK, the Multiple Sclerosis Society and the Cystic Fibrosis Trust, which say that patients now have to go to hospital to be allowed access to physiotherapy services that previously were freely available to everyone. The Department of Health has said: 'Efficiency savings should not affect important patient services, at a time when the budget is increasing by a total of £11.5 billion over the next four years.'

There is concern from the CSP that the government's revised NHS reforms will increase open market competition in the health service. Therefore they have asked that anything that could be deemed to promote competition should be completely removed from the reform proposals in order to ensure fairness. They submitted an official response to a scrutiny committee of MPs following a review by the independent NHS Future Forum. They said that the Bill will mean there is an 'open market' for healthcare providers which could harm patient services. That said, they welcomed the government's decision to widen the range of clinicians involved in the commissioning process. However, it is still the case that there are no compulsory positions on these new commissioning bodies for allied health professionals.

Workout at Work Day

In 2011, as a result of a survey from the CSP that found that four in 10 people get out of breath walking up stairs or running for a bus, the CSP launched Workout at Work Day on 8 September, with physiotherapists running events to get employees up and moving. The aim was to demonstrate the need for healthier habits and to build more activity into people's daily working lives. It was organised for 8 September to coincide with World Physical Therapy Day.

Physiotherapists held events in around 150 workplaces, from John Lewis stores, offices and hospitals to a power station. Employees were offered Pilates classes, lunchtime walking clubs, cycling challenges and table tennis, as well as advice and information sessions. It gave physiotherapists the opportunity to show what they can offer in occupational health terms and also to demonstrate the benefits of daily exercise in everyday life.

Alternative therapies

Physiotherapists are now becoming increasingly interested in utilising so-called 'alternative therapies' alongside traditional techniques. These can include:

- acupuncture
- Alexander technique
- aromatherapy
- chiropractic medicine
- massage
- reflex therapy.

Acupuncture

Acupuncture originated over 3,000 years ago in China. The practitioner inserts thin needles into the body at designated places in order to help alleviate or cure problems. Nowadays, this may also involve small electric currents. It is thought that the needles stimulate the body's nervous system into producing its own painkilling substances. The safe delivery of acupuncture is monitored by the Acupuncture Association of Chartered Physiotherapists (AACP), a clinical interest group of the CSP.

Alexander technique

The Alexander technique is a method of releasing unwanted muscular tension throughout the body by making the patient aware of balance, posture and coordination while performing everyday actions. It is particularly associated with the performing arts.

Aromatherapy

Aromatherapy uses essential oils that are derived from plants and flowers. The oils are either vaporised and inhaled, or applied directly to the body – often in conjunction with massage.

Chiropractic medicine

Chiropractic medicine aims to address the improper alignment of the vertebrae in the spine, which, it is believed, causes a number of physical disorders. Re-alignment is achieved by manipulation.

Massage

Massage is the manipulation of the soft parts of the body. Physiotherapists with a particular interest can do postgraduate training in many different types of massage. The CSP has a special interest group: Chartered Physiotherapists Interested in Massage and Soft Tissue Therapies (CPMaSTT).

Reflex therapy

Reflex therapy deals with problems within the body by targeting related points on, for example, the feet, hands or head. Reflex therapy can be arranged by consulting a chartered physiotherapist who is a member of the Association of Chartered Physiotherapists in Reflex Therapy (ACPIRT), the clinical interest group of the CSP.

7| Massaging the results
Results day

The A level results will arrive at your school on the third Thursday in August. The universities will have received them a few days earlier. You must make sure that you go into school on the day the results are published. Do not wait for the results slip to be posted to you. Get your teachers to tell you the news as soon as possible, once they are able to of course! If you need to act to secure a place you may have to do so quickly. The following paragraphs take you through the steps necessary to use the UCAS Extra, Clearing and Adjustment systems. They also explain what to do if your grades are disappointing.

The university admissions departments are well organised and efficient, but they are staffed by human beings. If there were extenuating circumstances that could have affected your exam performance and which were brought to their notice in June, it is a good idea to ask them to review the relevant letters shortly before the exam results are published.

If you previously received a conditional offer and your grades equal or exceed that offer, congratulations! You can relax and wait for your chosen university to send you joining instructions.

> One word of warning: you cannot assume that grades of AAC satisfy an ABB offer. This is especially true if the C grade is in biology. Always check with your chosen university.

What to do if you have no offer

If all of the universities that you applied to reject you, you are then eligible to enter a scheme called UCAS Extra. This allows you to apply to other universities, either for physiotherapy or for other courses. You will automatically be sent details by UCAS.

UCAS Extra starts in March. If UCAS Extra does not provide you with an offer, you can enter Clearing in August. These days very few applicants get into university through Clearing. Very few universities have spare places in August and, of those that do, most will choose to allow applicants who hold a conditional offer to slip a grade rather than dust off a reserve list of those they interviewed but did not make an offer to. Still less are they likely to consider applicants who appear out of the blue, however high their grades. That said, it is likely that every summer one or two universities will have enough unfilled places to consider a Clearing-style application.

If you hold, say, AAB but were rejected when you applied through UCAS, you need to let the universities know that you are out there. The best way to do this is by email. If you live nearby you can always deliver a letter in person, talk to the office staff and hope that your application will stand out from the rest.

Below you will find a sample email. Do not copy it word for word! Do not forget that your UCAS referee may be able to help you. Try to persuade him or her to ring the admissions officers on your behalf – your referee will find it easier to get through than you will. If your head teacher is unable or unwilling to ring, then he or she should at least email a note in support of your application. It is best if both emails arrive at the university at the same time.

From: Lucy Johnson
To: mdwhyte@melchester.ac.uk
Subject: Physiotherapy places

Dear Miss Whyte
UCAS No 07-123456-8

I have just received my A level results, which were: Biology B, Chemistry B, English C. I also have an A grade in AS Photography. You may remember that I applied to Melchester but was rejected after interview/was rejected without an interview. I am still very keen to study physiotherapy at Melchester and hope that you will consider me for any places that may now be available. My head teacher supports my application and is faxing you a reference. Should you wish to contact him, the details are: Mr C Harrow, tel: 0123 456 7891, fax: 0123 456 7892. I can be contacted at the above email address and could attend an interview at short notice.

Lucy Johnson

If you are applying to a university that did not receive your UCAS application, ask your head to email or send a copy of the application. In general it is best to persuade the university to invite you to arrange for the UCAS application to be sent.

If, despite your most strenuous efforts, you are unsuccessful, you need to consider applying again (see page 66). The alternative is to use the Clearing system to obtain a place on a degree course related to physiotherapy and hope to be accepted on a physiotherapy course after you graduate. This option is described on page 63.

What to do if you hold an offer but miss the grades

If you have only narrowly missed the required grades (this includes the AAC grade case described above) it is important that you and your referee email the university to put your case before you are rejected. Another sample email follows below.

From: Lucy Johnson
To: mdwhyte@melchester.ac.uk
Subject: A level results

Dear Miss Whyte
UCAS No 07-123456-8

I have just received my A level results, which were: Biology B, Chemistry B, English C. I hold a conditional offer from Melchester of ABB and I realise that my grades fall below that offer. Nevertheless, I am still determined to study physiotherapy and I hope you will be able to find a place for me this year. I would like to remind you that at the time of the exams I was recovering from glandular fever. A medical certificate was sent to you in June by my head teacher.

My head teacher supports my application and is faxing you a reference. Should you wish to contact him, the details are: Mr C Harrow, tel: 0123 456 7891, fax: 0123 456 7892. I can be contacted at the above email address and could attend an interview at short notice.

Lucy Johnson

What if your grades are significantly better than anticipated?

UCAS has introduced a new scheme called Adjustment, which is aimed at applicants who have achieved grades better than predicted. It is primarily designed for students who might have been predicted low grades and who, therefore, applied for those university places that would accept them rather than where they really wanted to go. The Adjustment system allows these students to hold on to their offers for a short period while contacting other universities where the standard offers are higher to see whether they can be considered. Full details can be found on the UCAS website.

Retaking your A levels

The grade requirements for retake candidates are often higher than for first-timers. You should contact the universities to find out what they require from retake students. Many A levels can be retaken in January, but this depends on the board as well as the subject. The school or college where you will sit the retakes will be able to help you. The timescale for your retake will depend on:

- the grades you obtained first time
- the examination board through which you studied.

If you simply need to improve one subject by one or two grades and can retake the exam on the same syllabus in January, then the short retake course is the logical option. If, on the other hand, your grades were DDE and you took your exams through a board that has no mid-year retakes you probably need to spend another year on your retakes. You would find it almost impossible to master syllabus changes in three subjects and achieve an increase of nine or 10 grades within the 17 weeks or so that are available for teaching between September and January.

Independent sixth-form colleges provide specialist advice and teaching for students considering A level retakes. Interviews to discuss this are free and carry no obligation to enrol on a course, so it is worth taking the time to talk to their staff before you embark on A level retakes.

Re-applying to university

The choice of universities for your UCAS application is going to be narrower than it was the first time round. Do not apply to the universities that discourage retakers unless there really are special extenuating circumstances to explain your disappointing grades. The following are examples of excuses that would not be regarded by admissions tutors as extenuating circumstances.

- 'I was revising on my dad's yacht and my files got soaked when I accidentally dropped them in the sea.'

- 'I left my bag on the bus the week before the exams, and all of my notes were in it, so I couldn't do any revision.'
- 'We moved house a month before the exams and a removal man trod on my notes, so I couldn't revise properly from them.'

Some reasons are acceptable to even the most fanatical opponents of retake candidates:

- your own illness
- the death or serious illness of a very close relative.

These are just guidelines, and the only safe method of finding out if a university will accept you is to write and ask them. A typical email is set out at the bottom of this page. Do not follow it word for word and do take the time to write to several universities before you make your final choice.

Notice that the format of your email should be:

- opening paragraph
- your exam results: set out clearly, with no omissions
- any extenuating circumstances: a brief statement
- your retake plan: including the timescale
- a request for help and advice
- closing paragraph.

Make sure that your email is brief, clear and well presented. Even if you go to this trouble, the pressure on universities in the autumn is such that you may receive no more than a standard reply to the effect that, if you apply, your application will be considered. Apart from the care needed in making the choice of university, the rest of the application procedure is as described in the first part of this book.

From: Lucy Johnson
To: mdwhyte@melchester.ac.uk
Subject: Application for physiotherapy

Dear Miss Whyte
Last year's UCAS No. 07-123456-8

I am writing to ask your advice because I am about to complete my UCAS application and would very much like to apply to Melchester. You may remember that I applied to you last year and received an offer of BBB/was rejected after interview/was rejected without an interview. I have just received my A level results, which were: Biology B, Chemistry C, English E. I was aged 17 years and six months at the time of taking these exams.

I plan to retake biology in January after a 17-week course and English over a year. If necessary, I will retake chemistry in the period from January to June. I am confident that I can push these subjects up to ABB grades overall.

What worries me is that I have heard that some universities do not consider retake candidates even when the exams were taken under the age of 18 and relatively high grades were obtained. I am very keen not to waste a slot on my UCAS form (or your time) by applying to departments that will reject me purely because I am retaking.

I am very keen to come to Melchester, and would be extremely grateful for any advice that you can give me.

Lucy Johnson

8 | The fifth metatarsal
Non-standard applications

So far, this book has been concerned with the 'standard' applicant: the UK resident who is studying at least two science subjects at A level and who is applying from school or who is retaking immediately after disappointing A levels. This chapter outlines the application process for 'non-standard' applicants.

The main non-standard categories are as follows.

Students who have not studied science A levels

If you decide that you would like to study physiotherapy after having already started on a combination of A levels that does not fit the subject requirements for entry to university, you have three choices.

1. You can spend an extra year studying science A levels at a sixth-form college that offers one-year AS/A2 courses. You should discuss your particular circumstances with prospective colleges in order to select suitable courses. It is worth being aware that only very able students can cover A level Chemistry and Biology in a single year with good results.
2. You can follow a Foundation course at a university that will then allow you to study a related degree course afterwards. For details of Foundation courses you should contact universities.
3. You can enrol on an Access course which is recognised by the universities you wish to apply to. Each university will have different policies about Access courses – you should contact the physiotherapy departments directly.

International students

The competition for the few places available to non-EU students is fierce and you would be wise to discuss your application informally with the university before submitting it. In general, overseas applicants will find it difficult to gain a place unless they can offer qualifications that are recognised by the universities, such as A levels or the International Baccalaureate (IB).

Information about qualifications can be obtained from British Council offices, British embassies and the universities that offer physiotherapy courses. Overseas students are liable for the full cost of tuition. For physiotherapy the fees vary depending on the university, but will be in the region of £12,000 per year. The UCAS website has a section for international students which describes in detail the application process and deadlines.

English language qualifications

In order to begin a university degree in this country, you are required to have an accredited English language qualification if you are a European or international student. This is essential so that you are able to understand the course and what is being taught to you throughout your degree.

You should be looking at achieving at least IELTS (International English Language Testing System) 6.5 to 7.0 in order to begin the university course and certainly no less than 6.5 in each band. Most universities will set this boundary higher in order to discourage some applications. If you would like further information on IELTS, please visit www.ielts.org.

TOEFL (Test of English as a Foreign Language) is also acceptable and you should be looking at a score in excess of 100 out of 120. If you would like further information on TOEFL, please visit www.ets.org/toefl.

Mature students

Physiotherapy courses are popular with older students, and the universities tend to have a flexible and encouraging approach to students over the age of 21.

Approximately 30% of students studying physiotherapy are mature students. Work experience is key as it points to you being a strong candidate and having researched the course properly.

Graduates

A 2.i degree (or higher) along with at least a grade B in A level Biology is normally required for graduates applying for physiotherapy. Most universities ask graduates to take a year out between the final year of their first degree course and the start of the physiotherapy course in order to get work experience. This allows them to demonstrate that they are serious about a career in physiotherapy.

Applicants with no suitable academic qualifications

Candidates are likely to be asked to sit at least two A levels, one of which will be biology, and to achieve B grades or higher. There are also some Access courses that can lead to an offer of a place to study physiotherapy; applicants should liaise with universities to confirm suitability.

The main difficulty facing those who come late to the idea of studying physiotherapy is that they rarely have a scientific background. They face the daunting task of studying science A levels and need very careful counselling before they embark on what will, inevitably, be quite a tough programme. Independent sixth-form colleges provide this counselling as part of their normal interview procedure.

Students not studying A levels

As with A levels, entrance requirements will vary from university to university. The information below is given as a guideline only.

- **BTEC Higher National Diploma:** 16 units, mostly biology or life sciences, with merits and distinctions throughout.
- **BTEC National Certificate:** 18 units, mostly biology and life sciences, with merits and distinctions throughout; plus one A level or two AS levels. The rules are tightening up on requirements relating to the BTEC and it is now common for you to need to achieve a distinction and have at least A level Biology as well.
- **Advanced Vocational Certificate of Education:** 12 units with science or healthcare-related options, possibly with one A level or two AS levels.
- **Irish Leaving Certificate:** six papers taken at one sitting, at Higher level, to include at least AABBB, or 400+ points.
- **Scottish Highers:** 300 points, to include two sciences.
- **IB:** 32 points with biology at Higher level (see Table 4).

Other qualifications, such as the European Baccalaureate, the French Baccalaureate or Open University qualifications, or the successful completion of a recognised Access course, will usually be considered but this is no guarantee that an offer will be made.

Access courses

A proportion of colleges of further education offer Access courses suitable for physiotherapy. The best known and most successful of these is the course at the College of West Anglia in King's Lynn. Primarily (but not exclusively) aimed at health professionals, the Access to Science and Nursing course lasts one year and covers:

- human biology
- forensic science
- health and community studies
- physics
- chemistry
- psychology
- geography
- level 3 mathematics.

The course might be Access to Science, to Health Studies, Physiotherapy or Medical Sciences, but you must cover cardiovascular, pulmonary and skeletal muscle physiology at level 3. Some universities will ask for biology or human biology. You should make contact with the specific institution to find out exactly which Access course they recognise.

You should contact the university admissions tutors or look on the university websites for advice. There is a strong case to suggest that those people getting in to universities are the ones who put in the work beforehand by talking to the universities. If you have a question, ask it – you will get an answer that you can then base your decision on.

9| Make no bones about it
Fees and funding

The following sections explain what the governmental changes mean in respect to university tuition fees and give you some ideas of where you might find help to fund your studies.

Fees

UK students

As a result of recent governmental changes, universities are allowed to charge UK and EU students up to £9,000 a year for tuition fees. This compares with a single fee for 2011 entry of £3,375. Most of the higher ranked universities will charge the maximum amount. The average course fee across all institutions will be £8,393. You should refer to the websites of the specific universities to find out what they intend to charge, and also the UCAS website, on the course search facility.

If you are a student resident in England you will pay up to £9,000 wherever you study in the UK. If you are a student resident in Scotland you will not pay any tuition fees if you study at a Scottish university. You will pay up to £9,000 if you study elsewhere in the UK. If you are a student resident in Wales you will pay up to £9,000 wherever you study in the UK. However, you will be able to receive a £3,465 loan from the Welsh government, and you will also be eligible for a grant up to the difference between the loan and the full fee. If you are a student resident in Northern Ireland you will pay up to £9,000 if you study in England, Wales or Scotland, but you will pay only £3,465 if you study in Northern Ireland.

EU students

If you are an EU student you will pay up to £9,000 if you study in England or Northern Ireland, but no fee if you study in Scotland. You will receive the same help as Welsh students (see above) if you are studying at a Welsh university.

Non-EU international students

The fees for non-EU international students do not have a set upper limit. The fees will depend on the course and the university. For example, Manchester Metropolitan University charges £11,640 per year, while Brunel will charge £11,765 per year.

Bursaries, sponsorship and grants

NHS bursaries

Students studying physiotherapy are eligible for a means-tested NHS bursary to help with any day-to-day living costs. The bursary usually covers the course fees and other practical costs. All new and prospective students are eligible to apply and students who are awarded these bursaries can also apply for student loans.

Applications checklist (according to the NHS Business Services Authority)

- Regardless of nationality, you must be considered to be ordinarily living in the UK and/or a UK country, as well as being settled in the UK under the Immigration Act 1971.
- In order to apply for the bursary, you must be given a conditional or unconditional offer at any university or higher education institution in England (other countries will apply the same conditions to their specific universities).
- Once your details have been received, the university or higher education institution will pass them on to NHS Student Bursaries, which will then contact you with your student reference number and information on where you can obtain the relevant application form on their website.
- From the academic year 2009/10 onwards, all students applying for a bursary are required to submit original documentation with their forms, i.e. a driver's licence or a passport.
- Applications should be submitted as soon as possible. The NHS bursary application form should be submitted within nine months of the first day of the course. For example, if your first day is 1 September 2012, then the last date when you can submit the application form is 31 May 2013.

To give you an indication of how much you might be eligible for, please refer to Table 3, which is published by the NHS Business Services Authority.

Home students and EU citizens who are not in receipt of an NHS bursary will be required to self-fund.

Table 3: Guideline student bursary eligibility (basic bursary rates 2011–12)

If you are studying:	During term time, You may receive up to:
At a university located **in London** and you will be living in student/rented accommodation or your own home	£6,928
At a university located **elsewhere in the UK** and you will be living in student/rented accommodation or your own home	£4,950
At a university located anywhere in the UK (including London) and you will be **living with your parent or parents** in their home	£3,838

Contact details for awarding bodies

England
NHS Student Grants Unit
Email: enquiries@nhspa.gov.uk
Website: www.nhsbsa.nhs.uk/Students.aspx

Wales
NHS (Wales) Student Awards Unit
Website: www.nliah.wales.nhs.uk

Scotland
Student Awards Agency for Scotland
Website: www.saas.gov.uk

Northern Ireland
Department for Employment and Learning Student Finance Branch
Email: studentfinance@delni.gov.uk
Website: www.delni.gov.uk

Sponsorship

Sponsorship is also sometimes available from prospective future employers; the Armed Forces are particularly well known to support students through their training. If you wish to apply for sponsorship from a specific sports club or national body – and bear in mind that quite a few of them will not advertise such schemes – then it is often best to get in touch personally in writing, stating your aims and career aspirations and the course on which you have been accepted to study.

Maintenance grant

In England, you can apply for a maintenance grant in order to cover the cost of your living costs. This is based on your overall household income. The maximum you can receive is £3,250 if your household income is less than £25,000. In Scotland there are different types of grants available: the Dependants' Grant (£2,640) or the Lone Parents' Grant (£1,305).

Universities charging more than £6,000 must provide financial support for students from disadvantaged backgrounds. You can find out about this at:

- www.ucas.com/students/studentfinance or
- www.direct.gov.uk/en/EducationAndLearning/UniversityAndHigherEducation/StudentFinance/index.htm.

National Scholarship Programme (for students resident in England)

Students whose family's income is less than £25,000 per year will be eligible for help from the National Scholarship Programme (NSP). This can take the form of help with either tuition fees or accommodation or other costs. The university will pay the scholarship and so the nature and size of the scholarship will vary from institution to institution. You can find out more about this at www.bis.gov.uk/assets/biscore/higher-education/docs/n/11-730-national-scholarship-programme-year-one.

10| Exercise the mind
Useful information and further resources

You are advised to check the UCAS Handbook or website for information on courses and universities before applying.

Universities offering physiotherapy degrees

University of Birmingham
Tel: 0121 415 8900
Website: www.birmingham.ac.uk

Bournemouth University
Tel: 01202 524111
Website: www.bournemouth.ac.uk

University of Bradford
Tel: 01274 233081
Website: www.brad.ac.uk

University of Brighton
Tel: 01273 600900
Website: www.brighton.ac.uk

Bristol, University of the West of England
Tel: 0117 32 83333
Website: www.uwe.ac.uk

Brunel University
Tel: 01895 265265
Website: www.brunel.ac.uk

Cardiff University
Tel: 029 2087 9999
Website: www.cardiff.ac.uk

University of Central Lancashire
Tel: 01772 892400
Website: www.uclan.ac.uk

Coventry University
Tel: 024 7688 7688
Website: www.coventry.ac.uk

University of Cumbria
Tel: 01524 384444 (Lancaster)
Tel: 01228 400300 (Carlisle)
Tel: 01539 430274 (Ambleside)
Tel: 01768 893400 (Newton Rigg, Penrith)
Tel: 020 7364 6334 (London)
Website: www.cumbria.ac.uk

University of East Anglia
Tel: 01603 456161
Website: www.uea.ac.uk

University of East London
Tel: 020 8223 2835
Website: www.uel.ac.uk

European School of Osteopathy
Tel: 01622 671558 (Academic site)
Website: www.eso.ac.uk

Glasgow Caledonian University
Tel: 0141 331 3000
Website: www.gcal.ac.uk

University of Hertfordshire
Tel: 01707 284800
Website: www.herts.ac.uk

University of Huddersfield
Tel: 01484 422288
Website: www.hud.ac.uk

Keele University
Tel: 01782 734005
Website: www.keele.ac.uk

King's College London
Tel: 020 7836 5454
Website: www.kcl.ac.uk

Leeds Metropolitan University
Tel: 0113 812 3113
Website: www.leedsmet.ac.uk

University of Liverpool
Tel: 0151 794 2000
Website: www.liv.ac.uk

London South Bank University
Tel: 020 7815 7815
Website: www.lsbu.ac.uk

Manchester Metropolitan University
Tel: 0161 247 2000
Website: www.mmu.ac.uk

Northumbria University
Tel: 0191 232 6002
Website: www.northumbria.ac.uk

University of Nottingham
Tel: 0115 951 5151
Website: www.nottingham.ac.uk

Oxford Brookes University
Tel: 01865 484848
Website: www.brookes.ac.uk

Plymouth University
Tel: 01752 600600
Website: www.plymouth.ac.uk

Queen Margaret University, Edinburgh
Tel: 0131 474 0000
Website: www.qmuc.ac.uk

Robert Gordon University, Aberdeen
Tel: 01224 262728
Website: www.rgu.ac.uk

University of Salford
Tel: 0161 295 4545
Website: www.salford.ac.uk

Sheffield Hallam University
Tel: 0114 225 5555
Website: www.shu.ac.uk

University of Southampton
Tel: 023 8059 5000
Website: www.soton.ac.uk

St George's, University of London
Tel: 020 8672 9944
Website: www.sgul.ac.uk

Teesside University
Tel: 01642 218121
Website: www.tees.ac.uk

University of Ulster
Tel: 028 7012 3456
Website: www.ulster.ac.uk

York St John University
Tel: 01904 624624
Website: www.yorksj.ac.uk

Grade and subject requirements for 2012/13 entry

The grade requirements listed here are correct at the time of going to press. Contact the universities before completing your application to check that they are unchanged.

Table 4: Grade and subject requirements for 2012/13 entry

Institution	A2 tariff/grades*	A2 Biology needed?†
Birmingham	ABB/320 (IB 34)	Grade B
Bournemouth	340	100 points (or PE)
Bradford	BBB (IB 32)	Grade B
Brighton	BBB (IB 34)	Grade B
Bristol UWE	320–360	Yes
Brunel	ABB (IB 33)	Grade B
Cardiff	AAB (IB 27)	Grade B
Central Lancashire	ABB (IB 30)	1 science
Coventry	330	Grade C or above
Cumbria	300	Yes
East Anglia	ABB (IB 31)	Grade B
East London	300 (IB 26)	1 science
Edinburgh (Biological Sciences; used before an MSc pre-registration course)	AAA–ABB	Two from biology, chemistry, maths and physics
Glasgow Caledonian	BBB	1 science/maths
Hertfordshire	300	2 life sciences
Huddersfield	ABB	Yes or sports science/ PE
Keele	ABB (IB 27)	Yes

Table 4: Continued

Institution	A2 tariff/grades*	A2 Biology needed?†
King's College	ABB+AS or AA/ BB+3AS (IB 32 HL 5 in 2 Sci)	Yes, or 2 from Chemistry/maths/ physics/psychology
Leeds Metropolitan	280	1 science/maths at B
Liverpool	300 (IB 30)	Grade B
London South Bank	180	60.38%
Manchester Metropolitan	300	1 biological science
Northumbria	360–320 (IB 32)	Grade B in a health science subject
Nottingham	ABB (IB 34 HL Biol 6)	Grade B or PE at B
Oxford Brookes	ABB/ABbb	Grade B
Plymouth	300	Yes
Queen Margaret	AAB	2 from biology/maths/ chemistry/physics
Robert Gordon	BBB (IB 32)	2 sciences
Salford	BBB (IB 32)	Grade B
Sheffield Hallam	300	Grade B in biology or chemistry
Southampton	ABBb (IB 33)	1 science
St George's	ABB	Grade B + another science
Teesside	300	Grade B
Ulster	BBB+HPAT	1 science
York St John	300	Grade B

* Lower-case letters indicate additional grades required at AS level.
† Most universities will accept or even prefer human biology, and some will accept a biology-related subject (psychology, sports science or PE), in place of biology at A level. You should contact the university for details.
Taken from *HEAP 2012* (Trotman, 2011)

Useful resources

Chartered Society of Physiotherapy

An essential starting point is the CSP's website (www.csp.org.uk). It carries detailed information about careers in physiotherapy and recognised courses. The CSP also produces many useful booklets about physiotherapy. They can be contacted at:

Chartered Society of Physiotherapy
14 Bedford Row
London WC1R 4ED
Tel: 020 7306 6666

The CSP publishes a magazine, *Frontline*, aimed at practising physiotherapists. The magazine contains articles of interest and is a useful way of keeping up to date with current issues and new developments. There is also a large jobs section – a good way to make contact with physiotherapy practices if you are looking for work experience.

Other societies

The Irish Society of Chartered Physiotherapists' website address is www.iscp.ie.

The College of Occupational Therapists
106–114 Borough High Street
London SE1 1LB
Tel: 020 7357 6480
Website: www.cot.co.uk

The Society of Chiropodists and Podiatrists
1 Fellmonger's Path
Tower Bridge Road
London SE1 3LY
Tel: 020 7234 8620
Website: www.feetforlife.org

UCAS

For information on university applications contact UCAS (www.ucas.ac.uk). The UCAS website has a search facility that will enable you to check the latest entrance requirements for all universities that offer physiotherapy courses. Application materials can be obtained from:

UCAS
PO Box 28
Cheltenham GL52 3LZ

Other useful addresses

Department for Employment and Learning (Northern Ireland)
Student Support Branch
4th Floor, Adelaide House
39–49 Adelaide Street
Belfast BT2 8FD
Tel: 028 9025 7777
Website: www.delni.gov.uk

NHS (Cymru) Uned Dyfarniadau Myfyrwyr
2il Lawr, Ty Golate
101 Heol Eglwys Fair
Caerdydd CF10 1DX
Tel: 029 2026 1495
Website: www.wales.nhs.uk

NHS (England) Student Bursaries
200–220 Broadway
Fleetwood FY7 8SS
Tel: 0845 358 6655
Email: sbaccount@ppa.nhs.uk
Website: www.nhsbsa.nhs.uk

NHS Wales Student Awards Unit
3rd Floor
14 Cathedral Road
Cardiff
CF11 9LJ
Tel: 029 2019 6167
Website: www.wales.nhs.uk

For visually-impaired applicants
RNIB Physiotherapy Resource Centre
University of East London
Romford Road
London E15 4LZ
Tel: 020 8223 4950

Students Awards Agency for Scotland
3 Redheughs Rigg
Edinburgh EH12 9HH
Tel: 0300 555 0505
Website: www.saas.gov.uk

Useful websites

Examination boards

www.aqa.org.uk
www.edexcel.com
www.ets.org/toefl
www.ielts.org
www.ocr.org.uk
www.wjec.co.uk

Online physiotherapy information

www.emedicine.com/pmr/contents.htm
www.evidence.nhs.uk
www.lifemark.ca
www.metis-uk.com
www.naidex.co.uk
www.thephysiotherapysite.co.uk

University league tables

http://education.guardian.co.uk/universityguide
www.timesonline.co.uk

Work experience

www.physiotherapyworkexperience.co.uk
www.prospects.co.uk

Fees and funding

www.bis.gov.uk/assets/biscore/higher-education/docs/n/11-730-national-scholarship-programme-year-one

www.studentfinanceni.co.uk/portal/page?_pageid=54,1265897&_dad=portal&_schema=PORTAL

www.studentfinancewales.co.uk/portal/page?_pageid=616,6200692&_dad=portal&_schema=PORTAL

www.ucas.com/students/studentfinance www.direct.gov.uk/en/EducationAndLearning/UniversityAndHigherEducation/StudentFinance

Further reading

Books on careers/university applications

How to Complete Your UCAS Application, Beryl Dixon, MPW Guides/ Trotman

University Degree Course Offers: The essential guide to winning your place at university, Brian Heap, Trotman

Books on physiotherapy

There are numerous textbooks covering all aspects of physiotherapy. Most of these are aimed at undergraduates or physiotherapy professionals. The following will give A level (or the equivalent) students an overview of what studying physiotherapy would entail:

A Practical Guide to Sports Injuries, Malcolm T F Read, Butterworth-Heinemann

Principles and Practice of Physical Therapy, William Arnould-Taylor, Stanley Thornes

11 | Don't be bone idle
Glossary

CPD
Continuing professional development

CPSM
The Council for Professions Supplementary to Medicine

CSP
The Chartered Society of Physiotherapy

CTD
Cumulative trauma disorder

ESWT
Extracorporeal shockwave therapy

Frontline
CSP magazine

Gait re-education
Learning to walk with a normal pattern again

HPAT
Health Professions Admission Test (Ireland)

HPC
Health Professionals Council

Hydrotherapy
Using water in treating pain relief and illness

Infrared and ultraviolet radiation
To warm damaged muscles and speed up healing

IPE
Inter-professional education

MCSP
Member of the Chartered Society of Physiotherapists

NHS
National Health Service

OOS
Occupational overuse syndrome

PBL
Problem-based learning

PBPL
Practice-based professional learning

Personal statement
Part of the UCAS application (3,000 characters with spaces), aimed at persuading universities to accept your application

RSI
Repetitive strain injury

SRP
State registered physiotherapist

Tennis elbow
Calcification of a tendon

UCAS
University College Admissions System

Ultrasound
Using sound waves to break down scar tissue and reduce inflammation

WRMSD
Work-related musculoskeletal disorder

WRULD
Work-related upper limb disorder

Postscript

If you have any comments or questions arising out of this book, we and the staff of MPW would be very happy to answer them. You can contact us at the addresses below.

Good luck with your applications!

James Barton

MPW (London)
90–92 Queen's Gate
London SW7 5AB
Tel: 020 7835 1355
Fax: 020 7259 2705
Email: enquiries@mpw.co.uk

MPW (Cambridge)
3–4 Brookside
Cambridge CB2 1JE
Tel: 01223 350158
Fax: 01223 366429
Email: enquiries@cambridge.mpw.co.uk

MPW (Birmingham)
17–18 Greenfield Crescent
Edgbaston
Birmingham B15 3AU
Tel: 0121 454 9637
Fax: 0121 454 6433
Email: enq@birmingham.mpw.co.uk